THE TRUE BOUNDARIES
OF THE HOLY LAND

SAMUEL HILLEL ISAACS
1825 — 1917

THE

TRUE BOUNDARIES

OF THE

HOLY LAND

AS DESCRIBED IN NUMBERS XXXIV: 1-12

SOLVING THE MANY
DIVERSIFIED THEORIES
AS TO THEIR LOCATION

By

SAMUEL HILLEL ISAACS

Edited by
JEANETTE ISAACS DAVIS

CHICAGO
1917

ISBN 978-1-60135-805-9

IN MEMORIAM

To my revered father, Samuel Hillel Isaacs, the learned and pious author of these pages, and to my beloved mother, Miriam Hadassah Isaacs, whose tireless and unselfish devotion to his welfare made it possible for him to pursue his studies, this book is lovingly dedicated.

In the Divine economy, my dear parents, though living to an advanced age, were not privileged to enjoy the fruitage of their labors during life time. The sacred task of publishing this, my father's last work, was thus transmitted to me. May it then bear its author's message of abiding faith in the infinite love and wisdom of our Creator and stimulate others to bring to light the hidden treasures of our sacred literature.

Mrs. Benjamin (Jeanette Isaacs) Davis

Chicago, September, 1917 — 5678

5

FOREWORD

IN presenting this book to the public I have made every effort to carry out the author's wishes even as to time. He foresaw the great events that were transpiring during the closing years of his life and felt that the time had come to bring into the foreground the extent of Israel's inherited territory. It was my privilege during my annual visits to his home in Bath Beach, L. I., to assist him in his literary labors and to seek out and bring to him from libraries such data and references as I could obtain. Contrary to general opinion, in my readings I was astonished and delighted to find that non-Jewish travelers and explorers had found the land of Israel to be one of exceeding beauty, in some parts rivaling California in its scenic grandeur and climate, particularly in the north, the descriptions and illustrations being such as to fascinate a lover of nature.

The subject of the "rights of small nations" and "Palestine for the Jews" are now being discussed pro and con by some of the governments of the world; Jewish Congresses are being convened in various countries to express the views of their constituents in order that unified action may be taken at the Peace Conference to be held at the close of the war.

The author's expressed desire was that his researches in this field be published before the American Jewish Congress convenes so that those interested might become familiar with his conclusions. The time, then, is opportune as this Congress is scheduled to meet November 18, 1917, in Washington, D. C.

7

FOREWORD

My gratitude is herewith tendered to those who have by advice or suggestion assisted me in carrying out the wishes of my lamented father and to those who by subscription have made publication possible.

To such scholars as Prof. J. Benzinger, of the Theological Seminary, Meadville, Pa.; Mr. J. D. Eisenstein, of New York City, editor and publisher of the Hebrew Encyclopedia, etc.; Prof. Louis Ginzberg, of the Jewish Theological Seminary of America, New York; Prof. R. D. Salisbury, Dean of the Geography Department, University of Chicago, I feel greatly indebted for encouragement.

J. I. D.

FOREWORD TO THE SECOND EDITION

SINCE the publication of the first edition of this book which has been received in authoritative circles with high appreciation, such remarkable and important events have occurred in rapid succession, bearing upon the boundaries of Palestine (now synonymous with the Holy Land or the Promised Land) that it seems necessary to bring to the attention of our readers and to emphasize the fact that the boundaries herein laid down by our author are those of Numbers XXXIV: 1–12, and do not include all of the Scriptural allotments mentioned in other Biblical passages.

The text of Numbers XXXIV: 1–12, is the smaller area which Israel is to inherit — a *reduced* grant — to which he hopes to be restored. But this does not mean that his request for a Homeland must be confined to these boundaries; on the contrary, our author states "God's conditional promises are never abrogated, but are reserved for fulfillment, etc.," and, "the provisional passages relate to what will be (at some future time)."

The *extensions* of territory there indicated, our author names "Provisional Grants" because of a *proviso* in the context: "For if ye will but keep all this commandment which I command you to do . . . Then will the Eternal drive out all those nations from before you . . . Every place whereon the sole of your foot may tread shall be yours: from the wilderness (of Sinai) and the Lebanon, from the river Euphrates, even unto the Western Sea shall be your boundary." (Deut. XI: 22–24.)

In this larger territory are included those valuable pasture and farming lands east of the Jordan which were allotted to the tribes of Reuben and Gad and the half-tribe of Manassah; also such as were acquired by peaceful settlement or justifiable conquest up to the time of King Solomon who reigned over the Jewish kingdom which had reached its largest extent before the death of King David.

It will thus be seen that Biblical, traditional, and historic boundaries include a much larger area than is generally conceded to the Jewish nation. The restoration of a national Homeland to the Jews under the trusteeship of Great Britain seems to be no longer a mooted question since the issuance of the British Declaration and its endorsement by France, Italy, and other governments and by our great President, Woodrow Wilson; to which has been added the approbation of His Holiness, Pope Benedict XV.

The Supplementary Map (VIII) shows the boundaries of Israel's definite inheritance (Numbers XXXIV) as compared with the approximate extent of Solomon's kingdom which is well within the "provisional grants."

Whether part or all of this territory shall be assigned to the new Jewish Commonwealth will be decided by the wisdom of the great men of the World's Peace Conference now in session at Versailles, where, as our author so remarkably predicted in 1906, are "gathered together the master minds of the world, commissioned to consider the grievances occurring between nations and settle them by justice and right—not by arms and fight—such a Convention may favorably consider the just claims of Israel and find ways and means of restoring him to his land on such conditions as to satisfy all concerned."

J. I. D. [Editor.]

Chicago, February, 1919—5679

CONTENTS

LIST OF MAPS

BIOGRAPHICAL SKETCH OF THE AUTHOR

SAMUEL HILLEL ISAACS was born in the small town of Ratzk, Russian Poland, in June 1825. As a child he was very ambitious to acquire knowledge and his parents made many sacrifices for their son's education. When the boy grew to manhood, he studied under such renowned teachers as Judah Bachrach, Moses Leib of Kutna and others of prominence. At the age of twenty-two he emigrated to America, then considered the "golden land of opportunity," arriving in New York City, June 30, 1847.

The path of the young student was strewn with many difficulties. While he thirsted for knowledge, he was dependent on his own efforts for a livelihood. Without means and without friends he soon realized that he must learn a trade in order to maintain himself and become master of at least part of his time for religious observance and study. There were no night schools in those days for Jewish immigrants, nor any of the numerous educational facilities of later years and the young man at once set himself to the task of learning the English language by his own efforts, literally "burning the midnight oil" and often for economy using wrapping paper for writing exercises.

In those early days the Jewish population of New York City was limited. Accordingly Jewish hospitality to the stranger was a feature of every day life. Close friendships were formed, which endured to the end. Mr. Isaacs' perseverance and indomitable will soon brought results. At the end of two years, in 1849, he had met and won the beautiful Miriam Hadassah, daughter of Ezekiel and Cherna Filipowski who, with their family, were among the earliest arrivals from Russian Poland in America.

Mr. Isaacs had learned the cigar trade. A few years later he became the proprietor of a small cigar factory and was his own salesman. Step by step his industry and thrift carried him onward until he established himself as a wholesale leaf tobacco merchant, often traveling to the tobacco fields of Virginia and Connecticut to purchase his stock.

Samuel Hillel Isaacs soon became the center of a group of learned men whose greatest pleasure was to gather together for religious, scientific and philosophical discussion and he was often called upon to participate in public ceremonies of a religious nature. His venturesome disposition showed itself by a trip to the gold fields of California in 1850, from which he returned sadly disappointed. His deep religious fervor was manifested by his intense desire to journey to Jerusalem with his family to live there. For this purpose, Mr. Isaacs, accompanied by his wife and four children, sailed for London, England, in 1860. Encountering unexpected financial difficulties which prevented him from continuing his journey, they were compelled to return to New York City.

During all his vicissitudes, he was a scrupulous observer of his religion in and out of his home. He never abandoned his studies and often contributed to Jewish periodicals in Hebrew, Yiddish and English. Strong articles appeared from his pen on the vital questions of the day such as "Shechita" (the Jewish mode of slaughtering animals) and "Milath Gerim" (circumcision of converts). He took an active part in Hebrew and Jewish educational problems and was fearless and outspoken for the truth. Although of a naturally retiring and courteous disposition he did not hesitate to criticize faulty statements even if emanating from those high in authority.

In 1890, at the age of 65, Mr. Isaacs retired from active business life to a home in Bath Beach, L. I., accompanied by his ever faithful wife. A family of ten children had blessed their union, four of whom died in childhood. Their remaining four sons and two daughters were married and in homes of their own. Thenceforth, Mr. Isaacs devoted himself to study and original research.

His mathematical and astronomical studies led him to specialize on the Hebrew and secular calendars. In 1891 he secured the copyright for an ingenious scientific arrangement of "A Calendar for a Hundred Years" and "An Artificial and Perpetual Calendar, Old and New Styles with the Dominical letters for each year." These received high praise from the *Scientific American*, the U. S. Government Bureau and other noted authorities.

A later production which has not been printed is "A Civil and Ecclesiastical Perpetual Calendar" including a special "Table for Easter and the Movable Festivals." To this was added a *Perpetual Hebrew Calendar* which is so constructed as to answer all calendar purposes and is probably the only one of its kind extant. When the correctness of the Hebrew Calendar for futurity was called into question by a noted authority in a public lecture delivered in Philadelphia, Mr. Isaacs immediately contributed a trenchant and valuable criticism in its defense which was published in the *Jewish Messenger* of New York City.[1]

He was also a valued contributor to *Torah M'Zion*, a Hebrew monthly published in Jerusalem which reprinted in pamphlet form (1901–08) his monographs on "Maamar Hodshe ha-Shanah" (Essay on the Hebrew Calendar), "Maamar Petach Enayyim" (An Explanation of some Halachic Passages in the Talmud), "Teome Zwiya" (The Twin Fawns; Essay on Palestinian Geography).

It was after the first Hague Peace Convention that he was persuaded by friends to prepare for English Biblical

---

[1] September, 1896.

13

scholars his discoveries concerning the true boundaries of the Holy Land. With almost the vision of a prophet he outlined in his "Preface" such events as he foresaw would occur in the world's history. For years he laboriously gathered and prepared his material, his failing health making it ever more difficult. The loss of his beloved daughter, Hannah Rachel Phillips of Chicago in April 1899, and again the death of his devoted son, Prof. Archibald E. Isaacs, who was a noted surgeon of New York City, in March 1913, were afflictions from which he never recovered.

Feeling keenly the loss of his devoted wife, who passed away in November, 1913, Mr. Isaacs, then 89 years of age, was brought to his daughter's home in Chicago. Physically feeble, but with mental faculties unimpaired, he endeavored to forget his grief by continued study. He finished the revision of his manuscript on the "True Boundaries of the Holy Land" and began Part II of his "Teome Zwiya" with Maps (in Hebrew), which remained unfinished. At the ripe age of 92, after an illness of five months, he was called to his eternal home, January 10, 1917, and was laid to rest in the family plot in Mount Carmel Cemetery, L. I., (Kehillath Jeshuran, N. Y.). Surviving him are two sons, one daughter and many grandchildren and great-grandchildren.

With him life and religion were intertwined and could not be separated. Undaunted by surrounding conditions he lived in a world all his own into which he introduced at times companions of other cultures. His character may well be expressed in a quotation from the Midrash found on the title page of his scrap book of 1879:

> "Hast thou sense,
> What lackest thou?
> Lackest thou sense,
> What hast thou?"

Chicago, September, 1917 — 5678.

THE AUTHOR'S PREFACE [1]

OF all the great events that have occurred since the beginning of history—especially the rise and fall of the many ancient nations, kingdoms, and empires on the ruins of which other powers arose—none are so wonderful as those included in the history of one small nation, limited in numbers and in strength, which the mighty Powers, each in turn, persecuted and endeavored to destroy, but which has survived and is progressing. .

Yes! Israel has witnessed the rise and the annihilation of his successive persecutors, but he himself could not be destroyed. He is the owner and the student of the *Book* of prescriptions, which, when he observes them, renders *him* indestructible. He, too, had his periods of rise and decline; these were, in a measure, due to his obedience and disobedience of these prescriptions. Renegades have always been found among Israel who were, and still are, the cause of all his miseries, but the main body has remained steadfastly faithful, and that, in turn, has kept him in preservation.

A great truth was proclaimed to the world in the words of Jeremiah (XXXIII: 23–26) which it would be well for Israel's persecutors to heed. It is as follows: "And the word of God came to Jeremiah, saying, The two families which the Lord had made choice of (Judah and Israel), *even these hath He rejected:* and they (thus) provoke My people, that they should be no more a nation before them. Thus hath said the Lord, 'When My covenant with day and night be no more, when I will undo the appointed ordinances of heaven and earth, then also will I reject the seed of Jacob and of David, My servant . . . . for I

---

[1] Written in 1906.

will cause the return of their captivity and have mercy on them.' "

This is but one of the countless prophecies which assure the remnant of Israel of a glorious future—of a restoration to his God, to his Holy Land, and to the establishment of universal peace and happiness.

And, although the accomplishment of these prophecies is not yet in sight—for instead of "beating the swords into plough-shares and the spears into pruning knives," new guns for wholesale slaughter are being manufactured, navies of great magnitude are being built, and sectarian strife has not ceased—yet the extraordinary signs of the times, of a universal character, may justify the conjecture of a possible partial restoration in a near future. Such indications are: (1) The International Peace Conventions, which though yet but experimental, may in time become practical and achieve their purpose; (2) The prevailing spirit actuating the changes from autocratic and despotic government to constitutional authority—when these two movements for international peace and constitutional government become fairly well established, justice, liberality and toleration may be expected to dominate; (3) The awakened interest in the Holy Land, evidenced by the late explorations therein, which have opened the country to our view and have made it possible to trace its boundaries (as will be seen) after they lay hidden for nearly two thousand years.

In addition to the above, there is the *Jewish question*, which has assumed grave proportions; and the *Zionistic movement* which has become quite a power and is progressing. The contemporaneous origin of them all makes it appear as if they were intended to coalesce and produce great and good results. It is possible, for instance, that the Zionists, being recognized as a representative body, may present the Jewish question and their claims before some future Peace Conference for a settlement. Such a convention, where will be gathered the master minds of the world, commissioned to consider the grievances occurring between nations and settle them by justice and right — not by arms and fight — such a convention may favorably consider the just claims of Israel and find ways and means of restoring him to his land on such conditions as to satisfy all concerned.

Whether this salvation shall come to pass in the manner above described or by additional momentous events which may yet arise, — whether it be sooner or later, in either case it is important to know the boundaries of the territory which Israel would claim.

But above and beyond this, when in the Pentateuch there is an extra section of twelve verses, commanding and detailing the direction of the boundaries of the Holy Land which are at present unknown, it becomes incumbent upon us, for the honor of our sacred writings, to render this section intelligible as soon as the correct location is procurable, and patiently wait for the fulfillment of God's promises *in His own way*.

2

INTRODUCTION

THE only detailed descriptions of the boundaries on all four sides of Israel's actual inheritance are found in Numbers XXXIV: 1–12, and in Ezekiel XLVII: 15–20. The geographical names there designated have been changed so often since the Biblical era that they could not be traced to existing places. The early expositions of these Scriptural passages, therefore, were but conjectures. These differed widely from one another and none explained the text correctly or produced an acceptable outline of the territory.

Identification of all the places mentioned in the text seemed impossible. The Great Sea on the west, and the Salt Sea with the Jordan on the east were known boundaries; but the northern part of the western and eastern borders, and the entire northern boundary were forgotten and left to speculation.

In later years more has been learned. Major C. R. Conder (*Palestine*, Dodd, Mead & Co., N. Y., pp. 16–20) writes: "The famous American, Dr. Edward Robinson, is credited as the beginner of real scientific exploration of Palestine; he made his journeys in 1838 and 1852. Sir Charles W. Wilson's survey and travels in Palestine closely followed (1864–66), and his subsequent exploration of the Sinaitic desert in 1867 roused public attention to the neglected state of Palestine geography, and led to the planning and execution of the wonderful excavations at Jerusalem by Sir Chas. Warren for the Palestine Exploration Fund. No less than nine noted explorers separately did good work about this time. The survey of Western Palestine from Dan to Beersheba and from the Jordan to the Great Sea was begun by the Exploration Fund in

1872 and completed in 1877;[1] Moab and Gilead were surveyed by the same party in 1881–82. Farther north, Lebanon and Anti-Lebanon were previously explored by Drs. Robinson, Porter, Thomson and others."

As to Northern Syria, the French military expedition to Syria in 1860 resulted in a detailed map of the Lebanon. For the extreme north of Syria, we have the work *Cilicia*, by Dr. F. X. Schaffer, of Vienna, 1903, and the *Handbook of Asia Minor, etc.*, by Sir Chas. Wilson, 1905. A very important and elaborate work is that published by Humann and Puchstein, entitled *Reisen in Kleinasien und Nordsyrien*, 1890, with an *Atlas* by Kiepert; also, the researches of Ramsay, Massy, Hogarth and others which have all been accomplished within the last seventy-five years.

These explorers in publishing their works felt and responded to the necessity of stating the ancient as well as the modern names of the places they were describing. This greatly helps the Scriptural student in comparing names with those he can find in ancient Hebrew expositors or Targums, for the purpose of making correct identifications.

It was in this way that the present writer was enabled to identify many of the Scriptural landmarks for the border lines so as to complete the boundaries on all the four sides in a rectangular figure, as directed by the text.

Having given the subject careful study for some years, and having found a new path, clear of all difficulties and satisfying all conditions, the writer issued a pamphlet in the rabbinical language and mode of discussion, stating his views and reasons therefor. On submitting the same to a few friends it was their unanimous opinion that it should be published in the vernacular for the benefit of the Biblical scholars of the English-speaking world.

---

[1] The survey of Eastern Palestine has been begun by the German "Palaestinaverein"; the maps are not yet completed.

INTRODUCTION

Following this advice, the author feels confident that his work will be appreciated according to its merits by this large class of Biblical students and respectfully solicits full attention to the reasons given for departing from the sites chosen by the existing expositors, as well as for the elected substitutes. This is a new departure especially in the northern part, and, confessedly, a bold move; but good reasons are given for each deviating step, which, the writer hopes, will be conceded and the new arrangement welcomed.

[*Note:* — As the arguments advanced for the rejection of existing identifications of places as well as for our substitutes involve somewhat lengthy discussions, we gather all such discussions in a Supplement, to which the reader is referred, except in such cases where necessity requires immediate presentation. Quotations throughout are numbered in accordance with original Hebrew text.]

CHAPTER I

THE SOUTHERN BOUNDARY

AKRABBIM — ZIN — KADESH (MERIBAH) — KADESH BARNEA
HAZAR ADDAR — AZMON — BROOK OF EGYPT

W E will take up and follow the text of Numbers in
its order, pausing between the sections for deliberation and exposition; also introducing Ezekiel's additional
marks for the placing of the Pentateuchal designations:

Our text begins the circumdelineation of the boundaries
from the southeast corner of the Salt Sea which it designates to be the southeast corner of the land. Thus it
says: (Numbers XXXIV: 3), "and your *southern* border
shall commence at the end of the Salt Sea on the east;
(4) and your border shall turn south of the ascent of
Akrabbim and pass to Zin, and its extremity shall be at
the south of Kadesh Barnea; and it shall go on to Hazar
Addar and pass on to Azmon. (5) And the border shall
turn from Azmon unto the brook of Egypt, and its terminating points shall be at the (western) sea."

With this Joshua XV: 2 f is in general agreement. There
we read: "Their south border was from the uttermost part
of the Salt Sea, from the bay that looketh southward."
The starting point, the south end of the Dead Sea, is here
indicated more clearly.

The second point in the border line is the "Ascent of
Akrabbim." According to Robinson (*Physical Geography
of Palestine*, Boston 1865, pp. 17–53) this is apparently the
remarkable line of cliffs which crosses the Arabah (the long
valley running from the south of the Dead Sea to the gulf
of Akaba) six or eight miles south of that sea: (see the
description in Robinson, *Physical Geography*, p. 53). The

running of the border from its beginning unto the south of Akrabbim is in Numbers not mentioned but understood; in Joshua (XV: 3) it is given in detail.

But since the Hebrew word for "ascent" does not mean a "line of cliffs," but rather a pass through which one ascends to a mountain or a high plateau, modern scholars agree that the "Ascent of Akrabbim" is one of the passes that lead to the northern slope of the great Wadi el-Fikreh, and which afford communication between Edom and Judah. It is not possible to identify it with certainty with any particular pass. Both the Nakl es-Safa and the Nakl el-Yemen have some points in their favor.

From this pass which is on the north side of the border, the border ran westward in a *curved* line, as the Hebrew term וְנָסַב (ve'nasab) implies, and passed to Zin. Its extending point (the most southern point of the curve) was at the south of Kadesh Barnea.

The designation: "and pass to Zin" is very indefinite, if we take Zin as meaning the wilderness of Zin. This covers a large tract — where did the border pass? It is, however, probable that Zin here and in Joshua XV: 3 is a locality, a village which is situated in the wilderness of the same name and gave its name to the wilderness.

The third point in the border line mentioned in Numbers XXXIV is Kadesh Barnea, which is on the north side of the border, belonging to the territory of Judah. We learn from Ezekiel (XLVII: 19) that the southern border passed by the *waters* of *Meribah* ("contention"). This is the place where Miriam died, and where the event happened which resulted in the sentence on both Moses and Aaron, not to lead the Israelites across the Jordan (Numbers, XX: 12, 13). According to Numbers (XX: 1, 13; XXVII: 14, a. o.) the "waters of Meribah" were near Kadesh and in the wilderness of Zin. On the other hand Kadesh Barnea whence the twelve spies were sent out by Moses and whither they returned (cf. Numbers XIII: 3, 26; XXXII: 8, a. o.), is said to be situated in the desert of Paran.

This would lead to the assumption that the two Kadesh are two different places, one in the wilderness of Zin, the other in the wilderness of Paran, and that the border line passed near both of them. The wilderness of Zin then would be situated in the north or north-east of the desert of Paran.

Most of the modern explorers and scholars, however, think that there was only one Kadesh in this region. Since the wilderness of Zin was adjacent to the wilderness of Paran and Kadesh in any case situated in the northern-most part of the desert of Paran, they think it possible to assume that Kadesh was regarded one time as located in Zin, another time as located in Paran. The borders of these wildernesses were not sharp lines as our modern political boundaries.

Regarding the site of *Kadesh Barnea*, there has been much controversy. Not to mention the improbable opinion of Stanley who places it at *Petra*, Rabbi Josef Schwarz identifies it with *Birein*, on account of the remarkable similarity of the name. Robinson and others identify it with *Ain el-Weibeh* on the western border of the Arabah, about thirty statute miles south of the Dead Sea; but later Rowlands has fixed the true Kadesh at Ain Quadîs (cf. *Manual of Biblical Geography*, Rand McNally & Co., Chicago, p. 47). Ain Quadîs is located about thirty degrees thirty-three minutes North latitude, thirty-four degrees thirty-one minutes east longitude. (ib. Map p. 44.)

These explorers, as we have explained, were looking for and have chosen, respectively, *but one* Kadesh, whereat all the events above mentioned (and more) occurred, not-withstanding that one Kadesh is surnamed *Barnea* and located in the wilderness of *Paran*, while the other, without a surname, was situated in the desert of *Zin*.

If, however, we assume the existence of two different places named Kadesh, as I think we ought to do, we have to identify Kadesh Barnea with Ain Quadîs. To identify the second Kadesh with Ain el-Weibeh would be only possible if we accept Robinson's identification of the "Ascent of Akrabbim" with the line of hills crossing the Arabah south of the Dead Sea (see above).

Kadesh Barnea of Paran and Kadesh of Zin have their separate histories, as already noted. The different important events which occurred now in the one and now in the other wrought great changes in Israel. Their positions on the map and the reminiscences they carry fit them both to be on the border of the land of Israel.

From south of Kadesh Barnea the border "shall go on to *Chazar Addar*," (Numbers XXXIV: 5). Joshua (XV: 3) gives instead of this name two other places, *Hezron* and *Addar*, and adds a third place, *Karka*, to mark the border more definitely. The second of these places, Addar, is identical with Chazar Addar in Numbers XXXIV. The Hebrew word Chazar means "village," "hamlet," and is added to the name of several villages.

Our text in Numbers XXXIV continues: "from Chazar Addar the border shall pass to *Azmon*." None of all these places is known today.

From Azmon the border turned (curving now northwest) unto the *brook* of Egypt, terminating at the sea. "The brook of Egypt" was formerly believed to be the *river* of Egypt (the Nile), but this belief is now abandoned and all agree that it is the torrent called "Wadi el-Arîsh," coming from the south of and running into the Great Sea at thirty-one degrees ten minutes North latitude and thirty-three degrees fifty minutes East longitude, Greenwich.

CHAPTER II

THE WESTERN BORDER

THE GREAT SEA

"AND as the western border shall ye have the Great Sea for a border; this shall be your western border." (Numbers XXXIV: 6.)

Although the Great Sea is an unmistakable landmark for the western boundary, it will be noticed that the text does not appear to define how far north on the sea coast this border extends, or the point at which it terminates.

It is evident that the point assigned for the northern termination of the western border is the same as that allotted for the beginning of the northern border, but the text is, in this instance also, apparently indefinite. Thus, it says (ib. v. 7), "And this shall be to you the northern border: from the Great Sea shall ye mark out (or turn to) Mount Hor," without specifying the spot on that sea whence to turn to that mountain.

This indefiniteness created a subject for speculation. Various theories were advanced as to the situation of "Mount Hor" and the "entrance to Hamath," the next station, and therefore the northern boundary line of the Promised Land is drawn in a very different way by different explorers and scholars. In order to show at a glance the confusion existing in the locations assigned as the northern termination of the western border, these theories may be here summarized as follows:

(1) The old opinion:

"Mount Hor" is one of the peaks of *Mount Hermon;* "the entrance to Hamath" is the pass to Hamath through the Bukeia, beginning southwest of Mount Hermon; the turning point on the sea coast is accordingly directly west of Mount Hermon, so that a line drawn from that point extending eastward to Mount Hermon constitutes the northern boundary. The latitude of Mount Hermon, which is thirty-three degrees twenty-four minutes North, would thus be the northern extremity of the land. (See Map II.)

(2) R. Esthori Ha-Parchi, a celebrated traveler, 1322:

"Mount Hor" is identified with *Jebel el-Akra* (the ancient Mons Casius) on the sea coast near the thirty-sixth parallel north, between Ladikêyeh and Alexandretta, the border thence running southeast to Hamath, crossing the Bukeia, which is "The entrance of Hamath." (See Map III.) This extends the territory about one hundred and ten (110) miles farther north than the preceding theory.

(3) R. Joseph Schwarz, 1850, often quoted by modern explorers:

"Mount Hor" is identified with *Jebel Nuriyah* on the coast, at thirty-four degrees nineteen minutes North, thence the line extends across the Bukeia (which he also takes to be the "entrance of Hamath") to his Zedad. (See Map III.) This extends the border about sixty-three (63) miles farther north than the first theory.

(4) Robinson and Porter (also Furrer in *Zeitschrift des Deutschen Palaestinavereins* VIII, 27; Neubauer, *Géogr. du Talmud*, p. 9 and many other scholars).

"Mount Hor" is *Jebel Akkâr*, the northern and loftiest part of Libanus. The "entrance to Hamath" is the valley which intersects the Lebanon and the Anseiriyeh mountains, carrying the River El-Kebir (Eleutherus) into the sea. (See Map V.) This river is thirty-four degrees thirty-eight minutes North, thus extending their border eighty-four (84) miles farther north than the first mentioned opinion.

That none of these theories[1] can be accepted is shown in the annexed Supplement wherein each is separately treated. Here they are merely referred to as necessary for the continuation of our subject.

The question now forcibly suggests itself: Why does the text use such dubious expressions where its intent is to indicate and stipulate? It is to us mortals that the description is given —why is it so ambiguously worded as to be susceptible of all these differing opinions? The northern border is but *one line* drawn over *one place*.

This question becomes more striking in face of the full description bestowed in our context on the other three corners. (Numbers XXXIV: 3, 5, 9, 10.) Why should this northwestern corner, only, be so loosely indicated as to create this speculation?

Moreover, the text, in describing the northern border, says (v. 7): "From the Great Sea shall ye turn to Mount Hor." This mountain is also unknown. Each of our theorists designates the one which suits his idea, but the several mountains chosen lie in far different latitudes. According to them this text which is intended to indicate the wherefrom and the whereto, would be so indefinite as to assign two unknown points, the one for the ending and the other for the beginning of important landmarks.

Furthermore, our text, in describing the western border (v. 6) deviates from its own method of designating the other three borders, viz.: in the latter it expressly points out the places of their respective beginnings and endings (cf. vs. 3, 5, 7, 9, 10, 12), but in the former (v. 6) neither the beginning nor the ending is at all mentioned; it only assigns the Great Sea (coast) as the western border, and,

---

[1] The following may also be included:

Kasteren (*Revue Biblique*, 1895, pp. 28 ff):

"Mount Hor" means the mountain where the Nahr el-Kâsimîyeh (the ancient Leontes) bends to the west, and where Kalat esh-Shakîf is the most conspicuous place.

if that term be so indefinite as to be susceptible of four different distances, would not the border necessarily be likewise undefined?

These unsatisfactory conditions stirred me to investigation. After serious circumspection and mature deliberation I became convinced that the intent of our text is misunderstood, and further study led me to arrive at the following conclusions:

Verse six (6) which says "And as the western border, shall ye have the Great Sea for a border" ought not and should not be understood otherwise than the primal and simple import of the words signified, viz: *that the Great Sea (without reservation) shall be the western border;* in other words, the *whole* eastern flank of the Great Sea *from its southeastern to its northeastern corners shall be the western boundary of the land.* If any point on the coast, between these two corners, were meant, the text would surely have designated that point. As it did not, "the Great Sea (Eastern shore)" *in toto*, was meant.

By this exposition we have a clearly defined expression in our text. As the whole eastern coast of the Great Sea was assigned for the western border, this border is as clearly defined as the sea coast itself —both are one and the same line, beginning, extending and ending alike so that any additional mark for this border would have been superfluous while in the other three borders it was a necessity. This explains the textual deviation noted above and also proves our interpretation of that text to be correct.

The western border, therefore, begins at the south-east corner of the Great Sea where the brook of Egypt falls into it (which is also the termination of the southern border, v. 5); thence it runs northward, passing Mount Carmel, Tyre, Zidon, the Lebanons, etc., unto the northeastern corner of the Bay of Alexandretta. This entire eastern coast is the western border of the land.

And now verse seven (7) also is not a dubious expression but a clear indication: "From the Great Sea (i. e. the ending point of the western border) shall ye turn to Mount Hor," etc.

In this application of our text, the phraseology of the two verses is directly to the point and all the puzzling questions are solved.

As the above interpretation is none else than a strict literal translation of our text and is clear of all ambiguity it merits acceptance without further proof. But we have more positive evidence to prove that the western border extended as far north as we assert; namely, the landmarks for the northern border, as indicated by our text further on, could not be acceptably located by any of the theorists, as will be shown in the Supplement (Chapters IV, V); while in searching for them in *that* northern latitude, we identify them all, by ancient authority or modern discovery as may be seen in the following chapters. We invite the attention of the reader to the reasons given there for our identifications and ask for his unbiased decision.

CHAPTER III

THE NORTHERN BORDER

MOUNT HOR

"AND this shall be unto you the northern border: from the Great Sea shall you mark out for you (or turn to) Mount Hor" (Numbers XXXIV: 7).

We have already seen that the expression "From the Great Sea" implies the northeastern corner of that sea where the western border of the land ends and where the northern border begins; obviously, running eastward to the first landmark denominated "Mount Hor."

This appellation, combining as it appears, a common and a proper name, is introduced to represent the Hebrew "הֹר הָהָר" (which is also composed of two nouns) rendering the component "הֹר" (Hor) as a proper noun and the other component "הָהָר" (the mount) as the common name, the two connected producing the appellation "Mount Hor."

But this reasoning is based on wrong premises; "הֹר" cannot be a proper noun here, because in such combinations, especially in those referring to mountains, the common precedes the *proper* noun in Hebrew as well as in English; it is correct to say "Mount Hor" not "Hor the mount," which is implied by the accepted interpretation and which is surely awkward English, as well as awkward Hebrew.

But we find another interpretation which correctly represents the Hebrew designation: The *Midrash Rabba* and the *Midrash Tanhuma*, two ancient authorities, both explain this term in the same words as follows: (they question) "And what is "הֹר הָהָר?" (ans.) "A mountain on top of a mountain like a small apple on top of a big

30

one." (M. R. Numbers XIX: 9; M. Tanhuma, Hukkath
14.) Accordingly each one of the two components sig-
nifies "mountain" but "הֹר" is a modification to construct
the two into one appellative name: "*the mountain of* (or
on) *a mountain*" and may refer to any mountain of that
description that is met by the border line on its way.

Consequently, *Mount Hor* is a mis-translation: it should
be rendered *the double (or duplicate) mountain;* or, what
is more literal, *the mounted mountain.* However, for
convenience, the appellation "Mount Hor" will be continued in this article.

AARON'S MOUNT HOR

The fact that the mountain on which Aaron died is
also called by the same name (Numbers XX: 22–25, 27,
et passim) attests this assertion: that it is but a descriptive
name and may refer to any mountain of the same contour.
But the question here suggests itself: Why did the text
make use of a dubious indication in both cases, where
each of them ought to have been clearly indicated? It
may be said, in answer, that because the two mountains
are so far apart and each one is located between two *known*
landmarks, a mere description is sufficient to identify them.
But this is true only of the northern mountain, the one we
are now in quest of, which is located, according to our
interpretation of the borders, between two such conspicuous landmarks as will forever remain —namely, the
corner of the Great Sea on one side and the "entrance of
Hamath" on the other side.

Not so is the southern mountain of Aaron's burial: it
is placed between Kadesh and Zalmuna (Numbers XXXIII:
37, 41), both of which are unknown. No less than three
locations are proposed for Kadesh, as mentioned above,
(cf. *Bible Atlas*, Rand McNally, Chicago, p. 47), and
Zalmuna is also questionably identified (ib. p. 49). How,

then, can they be taken as indicators of another object, when they, themselves, are doubtful?

And, although Scripture designates both Kadesh and Aaron's Mount Hor as being located at the border of the land of Edom (Numbers XX: 16, 23), yet, as the western border of that land is unknown (cf. above mentioned *Atlas*, p. 45), so must they be.

This is indeed the case with the mountain in which Aaron was buried: its identity is now much questioned. Such explorers as Rev. Edward Wilton (*The Negeb*, pp. 127 ff.); Dr. H. C. Trumbull (*Kadesh Barnea*, pp. 132 ff.); Niebuhr, Pococke and others (quoted by Prof. G. L. Robinson, D. D., *Biblical World*, Chicago, February 1908) reasonably reject the identification of the traditional Jebel Harûn with Aaron's Mount Hor. Most of them advocate Jebel Maderah as its site. This mountain is located about twenty-five miles southwest of the southern end of the Dead Sea and would be on or about the center of a line drawn from that end of the sea to Kadesh Barnea (ib. p. 88).

To the reasons given by Robinson (ib. pp. 98, 99) for the rejection of Jebel Harûn, one may be added which in our opinion is more convincing, viz: it is stated (Numbers XX: 21, 22) "When Edom refused to permit Israel to pass through his border, Israel *turned away from him.* And they journeyed from Kadesh and came unto Mount Hor." This journeying and encamping at Mount Hor must have been in "turning *away from* him"; therefore it could not be Jebel Harûn which lies *within* the territory of Edom and is one of the peaks of Mount Seir which was given in inheritance to Esau (Edom) (cf. Deuteronomy II: 5) and the Israelites were forbidden to take even a footbreadth of their land (ib.).

That Jebel Harûn is not Mount Hor is a certainty — that Jebel Maderah may be Mount Hor is a slight possibility:

it somewhat resembles a double mountain, its "roof" being divided into two independent sections as described by the above mentioned Professor G. L. Robinson (*ibid.* p. 91). However, the burial place of Aaron remains unknown, and the question still confronts us.

But the most probable solution of this question is, that it was intended to have Aaron's sepulcher hidden from the world, as is also the sepulcher of his brother Moses (Deuteronomy XXXIV: 6), for the plausible reason that their tombs should remain intact and not desecrated by any idolatrous worship, church or chapel; or, perchance, that their remains be not carried away to some museum, as the mummies of the Egyptian kings —the aboriginal anti-Semites —were carried away (Pharaoh Rameses II himself among them) and placed in the museums of Cairo, London, Paris and elsewhere, for visitors to gaze upon their dried and crusted faces.

This is but one of the many instances where the God of Israel guards His lovers; for, while the mighty pyramids of Egypt were not safe enough to guard the remains of the tyrannical oppressors of Israel, a defenseless sepulcher in the wilderness is left intact to guard the remains of a scion of the oppressed.

Having defined the appellation of the two mountains and shown reason for the concealment of the southern mountain, it is next in order to find the location of the northern mountain which is assigned, not as a burial place, but as a landmark for the living, that *should* be known:—

The text, as before quoted, says: (Numbers XXXIV: 7) "And this shall be your northern boundary: from the Great Sea shall you mark out (or turn to) Mount Hor," etc. This starting point of the northern border is, as we have seen, the northeastern corner of that sea. It is further certain that the direction of this border line is eastward; consequently, this line will strike on its way the *Mountains of Amanus* (Amanus mons of the Ancients) which run near by, north and south. These mountains of Amanus contain our first Biblical landmark of the northern border, commonly called Mount Hor, as we will endeavor to prove by ancient and modern authority.

THE TARGUMS

The ancient Aramaic translations of the Pentateuch, called "Targum of Jonathan" and its compeer, "Targum Jerushalmi," both identify the Hebrew term (הֹר הָהָר) "Hor Hahar" with "Mount Amanus." The former renders that term by *Mount Umanis* in both the verses seven and eight of our text, and in recapitulating the cardinal four points of the boundaries (v. 12) it says: "Rekem Geya (Kadesh Barnea) on the south; Mount Umanis on the north; the Great Sea on the west and the Salt Sea on the east"; and the latter (Jerushalmi) renders the Biblical term of the two verses, *Mount Manos*, dropping the first letter of the name as was the characteristic trait of the Jerusalemites. The names: Liezer, Bun, Ba, are in vogue instead of Eliezer, Abun, Aba, respectively, on most pages of that Talmud. (See also Talmud B., Baba Kama, 6b.) This is plain and positive ancient authority for our position in identifying Mount Hor with Mount Amanus.

In offering these authorities as evidence, a little explanation as to their origin and characteristics may be required: "Targum" is an Aramaic word occurring in Ezra (IV: 7) and implies either "translation" or "interpretation." The former is mostly a literal, or word for word, rendition; the latter is more expanded in explaining the sense and conditions of the subject and is called paraphrastic. The *Targum* became an important and necessary institution during the Babylonian exile when the populace became accustomed to the Aramaic language instead of the Hebrew. The interpretation of the "Law" in public reading or private study was rendered in that language which was better understood, so phrased as dictated by authority.

We have three Aramaic Targums on the Pentateuch: "Targum Onkelos" which is a literal translation and the two others referred to above, called respectively "Targum Jonathan" and "Targum Jerushalmi." The former of the two is complete; the latter is extant only in fragments, placed in some verses beside that of Jonathan wherever the two somewhat deviate. It seems that these fragments were culled from a complete version which otherwise agreed with Jonathan's. However, both these Targums are paraphrastic interpretations, and even admitting the view of modern critics who place them as late as the seventh century, they may still be called ancient authority, for we must not forget that these interpreters were not beginners of the Targum institution, but only committed to writing that which was traditionally and orally known many centuries before. (See *Chambers Encyclopedia:* "Targum.") Certain it is that their transcriptions of geographical names are fully reliable.

There is another characteristic difference between Onkelos and the other Targums, viz: Onkelos retains the original geographical names which were changed in course of time and very seldom adopts the new form; Jonathan and Jerushalmi use the new names which were current during their own time. As an instance, we will cite the name of the country first mentioned in the Bible (Genesis II: 11), "The land of *Havilah*," which Onkelos copies, but which Jonathan translates "Hindike" (India), agreeing with Josephus (*Ant.* Book I, Chap. I). Likewise further on (Genesis X: 10–18) there can be seen many names which Onkelos gives in the original form, but which the other Targums render by the names known at the time of their writing. This characteristic trait runs through the whole of these editions and makes them the more valuable for purposes of identification. And for this reason they were the sources of information for all expositors and commentators.

In returning to our subject (Mount Hor), we find the same condition. Onkelos copied the Biblical term while Jonathan rendered that term by "*Mount Umanis*," and Jerushalmi by "*Manos*," as it was known and called by this name in their time. Therefore, we have ancient authority, as before said, for the establishment of our claim that *Mount Amanus* is a later name for *Mount Hor* which is *the first Biblical landmark of the northern border*.

THE TOSEFTA

Furthermore:—The "*Tosefta*," (which is a supplement to the *Mishnah*, redacted in the third century) in discussing the declivities of the border-mountain, is quoted in Talmud B. (Gittin, p. 8a), as follows: "All that is sloping down from Mountains Amanon (מִטּוּרֵי אַבְנוֹן) and *inward* is *Eretz Israel* (land of Israel); from the Mountains Amanon and *outward* is excluded. The islets in the sea are determined by an imaginary line drawn from Mountains *Amanon* to the Brook of Egypt; inside that line is included, outside thereof is excluded."

The term "טוּרֵי אַבְנוֹן" (Turey Amanon) mentioned here three times is decidedly Aramaic; "טוּר" (Tur) means "mountain" in that language, the ending (ֵ) makes it plural and construct with the following noun: "the mountains of Amanon"; for here it refers to a stretch of that ridge (as may be seen further on, when we mark out that boundary). "Amanon," then, was the primitive form of "Amanus" until the Greeks, who took possession of the land, modified the name into the Greek form; as they merged "Lebanon" into "Libanus" so they changed "Amanon" into "Amanus."

There can be no doubt that the mountains of *Amanon*

36

of the Tosefta are identical with the Mount *Umanis* or *Manos* of the Targums, and both with the *Mons Amanus* of the Greeks whose location along the bay of Alexandretta is undoubted, and justifies us in extending the western border to the northeastern corner of the Great Sea.

But, later on, the name of these mountains underwent an entire change. At present the mountains in question have no common name. The name *Amanus* was lost. It was superseded by *Alma Dagh* and *Giaour Dagh* which are still in use. The former applies to the southern part of the ridge and the latter to the part extending thence northward. This change must have taken place at or soon after the Arab conquest of Syria in the seventh century,—*Dagh* is a Turkish word and means "*mountain.*"

Thus may be explained why even some of our own expositors, knowing the *Umanis* and *Manos* of the Targums and the *Amanon* of the Tosefta, did not identify them with the similar name of Amanus; for now we can see that in their time (end of eleventh century and later) the name Amanus had been well-nigh forgotten by the general public, and they could find no other mountain similar in name except the Amanah of Canticles (IV: 8), which is a peak on Mount Hermon. And on the other hand, geographers and explorers who knew ancient Amanus did not know the connection of Mount Hor therewith as rendered by the Targums. They might have known the Amanon of the Tosefta as it is quoted in Talmud Gittin; but as the universal belief was, that the northern border crossed at Mount Hermon (see Supplement Chapter II), they, as well as the former expositors, also identified Amanon with the Amanah of Canticles and thus gave rise to the maps of Palestine in which Mount Hor is placed on Mount Hermon, the latter having been considered the northern border of the *Promised Land*. As further evidence that this conviction still prevails we have the map of Thomas

Starling, "Canaan or the Land of Promise," also the map of "Ancient Palestine" (in the work of Thomas Wright, mentioned in Supplement, Chapter II) where Mount Hor is placed on Mount Hermon and in Osborn's *Geog. Appendix*, p. 571 (also referred to in Supplement, Chapter II) Mount Hor is but another name for Mount Hermon.

From the last two writers and geographers we learn that this theory was beginning to be abandoned in their own time. The former adds to his map of "Ancient Palestine" one of "Modern Palestine" in which Mount Hor does not appear on Mount Hermon; and the latter follows the old identity with a question mark. It is most probable that this change was the result of the appearance of the writings of Robinson and Porter who placed Mount Hor farther north on Mount Lebanon (Supplement, Chapter V). However, since their time the maps of the Promised Land have assumed a new form, extending the land as far north as the valley of the Eleutherus, which is, according to them, "the entrance of Hamath": *Atlas Antiquus*, Henry Kiepert, 1892; *Bible Atlas*, Rev. J. L. Hurlbut, D. D. (Rand McNally, Chicago, 1899), *cf.* the Bible dictionaries, as Cheyne, *Encyclopedia;* Hastings, *Dictionary of the Bible; Jewish Encyclopedia;* and elsewhere. Their theory, also, is discussed and discarded (in same Supplement) for good and sufficient reason.

Finally, to complete the evidence of our identification of *Mount Amanus* with the textual term "הֹר הָהָר" (Hor Hahar), we should remember what was shown at the opening of this chapter, viz: that the two Midrashim establish the fact that this term is but a *descriptive* name and consequently may refer to any mountain of the same description. The contour required by the text is that of "a mountain on top of a mountain" and this is really the case with *Mount Amanus* (which is the modern Giaour Dagh), as recent explorations testify: Dr. F. X. Schaffer of Vienna ("Cilicia," *Petermanns Mitt.* No. 141, 1903, p. 94) says: "Der Giaour Dagh erhebt sich fast durchwegs über 1,000 M. und seine höchsten Spitzen erreichen 1,800 M." (p. 95) "Eine viel begangene Karawanenroute läuft von Osmanie nach Jarpuz (Dschebel Bereket), das der Hauptort des gleichnamigen Sandschaks ist *und 1,000 M. hoch mitten in den Bergen des Amanus liegt.*"

Here we have a conspicuous mountain on top or in the middle of another mountain, which tallies with the textual appellation and which the border line unavoidably strikes —Jebel Bereket on Mount Amanus —this completes the identification.

Thus, the Targums, following in the wake of the *Midrashim* and knowing the formation of Mount Amanus, *as told us by late exploration*, were perfectly justified in combining together the two facts and interpreting the textual *descriptive* term to refer to the mountain answering the same *description*, which is *Mount Amanus*, the so-called Mount Hor.

The "much traveled caravan-route" mentioned by our explorer,—running from Osmanie to Yarpuz —is also marked out on Kiepert's map (*Reisen in Kleinasien und Nordsyrien*, Humann und Puchstein, 1890), beginning at Alexandretta, passing northward east of the plain of Issus, and curving towards Osmanie, thence continuing to Yarpuz, and further on. This route may be identified with the "way of Hethlon" marked out by Ezekiel (XLVII: 15). As great routes in mountainous regions can seldom be changed, this route, also, might have existed in Ezekiel's time; and, according to this theory, "Yarpuz" may be identified with "Hethlon."

Or, which is more probable, "the way of Hethlon" may be the route beginning at the northeastern corner of the Great Sea running to Osmanie and thence to Yarpuz; in which case Osmanie would be identified with Hethlon. (See Map VII.)

CHAPTER IV

THE NORTHERN BORDER (Continued)

ENTRANCE OF HAMATH—ZEDAD

HAVING settled the great controversy about Mount Hor, we will now proceed to trace the succeeding landmarks. The text continues:

"From Mount Hor ye shall point out your border unto the entrance of Hamath; and the goings forth of the border shall be towards Zedad." (Numbers XXXIV: 8).

Two landmarks are here given and both require explanation. We will treat them in the order named, and begin with

THE ENTRANCE OF (OR INTO) HAMATH

The expositors before mentioned endeavored to locate this landmark at or about the *city* of Hamath. It will be shown (Supplement, Chapters IV, V), that their respective conjectures cannot be accepted. As, in *our* tracing of the borders, by the strictly literal meaning of the text, we are brought to the northeastern corner of the Great Sea for the northwestern corner of the land, and thence, by the authority of the Targums, we are brought to Mount Amanus (the modern Giaour Dagh) for the true location of "Mount Hor,"—so shall we succeed in our present quest by adhering to the literal meaning of the textual description and by searching for it in the vicinity of the Mount Hor (Mount Amanus) now identified:

"Entrance" implies a narrow, guarded passage for entering a place proximate to it; and, since this "entrance" is designated as a landmark for the boundary of very valuable land and for everlasting evidence, it must needs be an extraordinary entrance. Such really exists not very far from our newly found "Mount Hor." *It is the celebrated Pass across Mount Amanus* which answers all the conditions required, through which the border crossed that mountain, entered the territory of Hamath (which stretched out to northern Syria, see Supplement, Chapter VI) and passed through it eastward to Ziphron and Hazar Enan.

To show the exact location of the Pass and its importance, we quote the following from Sir Charles Wilson (*Handbook of Asia Minor*, 1905, p. 278), who says: "The Giaour Dagh, fifteen to twenty-five miles wide and not more than six thousand feet high, is a strong barrier. It is crossed by two good passes, the Baghche, through which a road runs from the Cilician plain to Aintab, and the Beilan..... Other tracks across are rough, difficult bridle paths."

A more detailed description of the Pass is given by John Carne, in *Syria, the Holy Land and Asia Minor*, (Fisher & Co., 1836, Vol. 1, p. 10). He says: "The celebrated Pass leading from Cilicia into Syria....is a remarkable defile through a chain of inaccessible mountains and admits of only eight horses abreast," etc. The same author also says (Vol. 3, p. 37): "this plain (the one from which the Pass begins) is an impressive scene, like one of those which we fancy to be marked by nature for some great event."

Now let us glance, for a moment, at our geographical position: Mount Amanus was the boundary between northwestern Syria (Syria Pierea) and Cilicia—Syria on the east of the mountain and Cilicia west of it. Eastern Cilicia which was bounded on the north by the Taurus mountains, extended over the western declivity of Mount Amanus, while the eastern declivity of the mountain was then "the land of Hamath." The pass from one to the other was *the most northerly entrance to Hamath from an* alien[1] *country*. This was very important in those ancient days of warfare and invasion by foreign races. It is therefore a conspicuous and well-fitted landmark for the border to pass over from "Mount Hor" which is in Cilicia across Amanus to the territory of Hamath, to the Lebanons, etc. Thus we have found the second landmark of *Numbers* on the northern border, "the entrance of Hamath."

ZEDAD

The next landmark requiring explanation is "Zedad"; and indeed there seems to be so much confusion concerning its location as to require careful deliberation. In following the order of the landmarks (proceeding from west to east) as given in our text of Numbers (XXXIX: 7-9), Zedad is mentioned after the "entrance of Hamath," and consequently would be located *east* of that place, while in Ezekiel's description Zedad is placed *west* of Hamath. Ezekiel says thus: "And this shall be the boundary of the land: on the north side, from the Great Sea, the way of Hethlon, to the entrance of *Zedad*; *Hamath*, Beirotha, etc." (ib. XLVII: 15, 16). "The way of Hethlon" is undoubtedly that which leads to or passes by Mount Hor which is not mentioned here otherwise; "Beirotha" is the ancient "Beroea," the modern Aleppo (or the territory of it). Thus we see that the direction of the border is here also eastward and yet Zedad is placed before or west of Hamath.

Moreover, the Targums of Jonathan and Jerushalmi both interpret the Zedad of our text "*Ablas de Cilicia*" which seems to be a mystery. To show the anomaly it is necessary to repeat the text: "From Mount Hor you shall point out your border unto the entrance of *Hamath*; and the goings forth of the border shall be to Zedad" (Numbers XXXIV: 8). How is it possible that the border,

---

[1] From Cilicia into Syria.

running eastward, and reaching Hamath which is at the *eastern* end of the Pass, should return back to Cilicia which is *west* of the Pass? These questions are very important and require a valid explanation.

Far be it from us to think that Ezekiel differs with the delineation of Numbers. Whenever two sacred texts appear to conflict with each other, we should conclude that either both of the texts are or one is not correctly understood and we should try to find the correct interpretation which will make them agree. In our case, Ezekiel's version is simply phrased, fixing the position of Zedad *before* or *west* of Hamath, and *cannot be changed.* But the text of Numbers is a sentence containing two clauses, the second of which modifies or defines the direction of the border given in the first clause: "From Mount Hor ye shall point out *your border* unto the entrance of Hamath" is modified by the second clause which says: "And the goings forth of *that* (same) border (i. e., between Mount Hor and Hamath) shall be towards Zedad," and, we have to add, *thence* to Hamath, that is, the territory of Hamath. (See Map VII.)

By this interpretation all that is said in verse eight about the border has no reference to its extension *beyond* Hamath and the texts are therefore in agreement that Zedad is located *west* of Hamath; and the seeming mystery of the Targums also disappears. *"Ablas de Cilicia"* which is the translation of Zedad, though mentioned after Hamath, was actually passed by the border before reaching Hamath.

To prove the verity of this interpretation we need but to take notice of the different terms used in our context in expressing any forward continuation of the border. They are respectively: "וְנָסַב" (ve'nasab) "and the border shall *curve out*" (Numbers XXXIV: 4, 5); "וְעָבַר" (ve'abar) "and *pass on*" (ib. v. 4); "וְיָצָא" (ve'yatsa) "it shall *go out*" (ib. v. 4, et passim), etc., verbs implying *action* or forward *motion*. But our (modifying) clause does not speak in such terms as signify action or motion. It does not say: "and the border *shall go out* to Zedad" (as in the following verse: "to Ziphron"), but says: "And the goings forth of the border *shall be* (in the Hebrew, "וְהָיוּ"—ve'hayu), towards Zedad" which is, evidently, only describing the track of the border spoken of in the first clause, which might otherwise be misunderstood. Thus, the first clause: "From Mount Hor ye shall point out your border unto the entrance of Hamath," might be understood to mean that the border shall run from one point to the other without interposition and in about the same direction (E. N. E. See Map VII) as it runs hitherto from the Great Sea, reaching the entrance of Hamath at the eastern end of the Pass, and excluding Zedad and the Pass from within the border. To avoid this misinterpretation follows the second clause: "And the goings forth of the border shall be to Zedad," i. e., the border shall now turn in a more northerly direction (See same map) and run unto Zedad, which is situated at the *western* end of the Pass (as will be seen) and, thence, through the Pass to Hamath, all of which is here termed "the entrance to Hamath" indicated in the first clause and which comes *after* Zedad, as Ezekiel places them.

We will now endeavor to locate Zedad. Ezekiel's expression is "lebo[1] Zedadah" and our text has the same for Hamath, "lebo Hamath"; and as the latter is universally (and correctly) interpreted "the *entrance* of Hamath" so should the former be rendered "the *entrance* of Zedad." This implies location at the *Pass* and as Hamath was at the *eastern* end of the Pass so must Zedad be at the *western*

---

[1] This term "lebo" is the more significant because it does not recur, in its construct state, except in connection with Hamath (five times) and with Zedad (but once).

end thereof (in Cilicia), thus agreeing with the exposition of the two Targums before mentioned.

Sir Charles Wilson (*Handbook of Asia Minor*, 1905, p. 278, quoted above) says: "The Giaour Dagh. . . .is crossed by two good passes, the *Baghche* through which a road runs from the Cilician plain to Aintab, and the Beilan. . . . .Other tracks across are rough, difficult bridle paths."

We thus identify Baghche, situated at the western end of the Baghche Pass, *with Zedad*, the northernmost point of the northern border, latitude thirty-seven degrees twelve minutes North.   (See same map.)

CHAPTER V

THE NORTHERN BORDER (Continued)

ZIPHRON (AFRIN)—HAZAR ENAN (AINTAB)

CONTINUING the northern boundary eastward, from the eastern end of the Pass, which is the modern village of Kazan Ali, our text says:—

"And the border shall go out to Ziphron, and its termination shall be at Hazar Enan: this shall be unto you the northern border." (Numbers XXXIV: 9.)

In the work entitled *Reisen in Kleinasien und Nordsyrien*, by Karl V. Humann und Otto Puchstein, 1890, (*Atlas* by Kiepert), Puchstein, page 115, describing the hills, valleys, etc., on the road to Oldje (going east from Sakchegözu to Aintab), says: "To the right, before us, stretches a *larger* valley (of the Afrîn) about N. to S. W., we overstep, in the plains, many tributary watercourses."

It appears, from the above, that this *larger* valley was known and called by the name of its principal river, the *Afrîn*. There is also a city of the same name, situated near the southern end of the river, as the following will testify:

In *Our Ride through Asia Minor*, by Mrs. Scott-Stevenson, 1881, map by Herbert Kitchener, R. E., we find the town of *Afrîn* described on the road from Alexandretta to Aleppo. Baedeker's *Palestine and Syria*, 1898, page 422, contains the following: "we reach *Afrîn*, situated on the river of that name (the ancient Ufrenus)."

Encyclopaedia Britannica, Volume 22, p. 281 says: "The Afrina (Ufrenus of the ancients) falls into Ak Deniz lake and so into the Orontes."

On the map, in *Syria, the Holy Land and Asia Minor*, by John Carne, the same river is called Ifrin.

Reviewing all the different forms of this name, and the large extent and importance of the valley of the Afrîn, at once leads us to determine that they all are derived from the primitive Biblical name "Ziphron" which is designated in the above quotation for the border to "go out to." And as our text names "Ziphron" only for the whole interval between the eastern end of the Pass and Hazar Enan, Ezekiel fills up the gap by assigning four places for the same distance.

These four places are Hamath, Beirotha, Sibrayim and Hazar Ha-tichom (Ezekiel XLVII: 16), and may be interpreted as follows:

(1) "Hamath," the territory of Hamath (in northern Syria as already explained).

(2) "Beirotha," the territory of Aleppo, which occupies the site of the ancient Beroea, a place of great antiquity. (cf. *Enc. Britannica*), and which also extended northward.

(3) "Sibrayim" and (4) "Hazar Ha-tichom," uncertain.

Although the last two places are not identified there is sufficient evidence from the first two for the direction of the border to go to Ziphron, the northern valley of the Afrîn, as before stated.

Targum Jonathan interpreting same verse also adds four places of different names the fourth of which is similar to Ezekiel's addition.

Furthermore, in describing the road from Kazan Ali (the eastern end of the Pass) to Aintab (*Handbook of Asia Minor*, 1895, by Sir Charles Wilson, pp. 275–6) the explorer says: "In the plain about one hour south of Kazan Ali is the mound," etc., "where the German excavations have exposed a large number of Assyrian, 'Hittite' and old Semitic monuments, and extensive remains of two or three palaces."

The same explorer further says: "After crossing the

Arslansi Ova, are several artificial mounds......Sakche
is a walled Konak, in which are *Hittite* sculptures. Following the east side of the plain we reach Konak Ghoja, an
ancient site, with remarkable rock-hewn chambers, a fine
spring....six artificial mounds, in some of which *Hittite*
sculptures have been found......Passing Sultan Oghlu we
join the road from Marash to Aintab at Benyak Arabler,
one hour before reaching *Sam* with a good spring in which
are sacred fish. Thence to Aintab (two hours)."

"The valley east of the Giaour Dagh (ib. page 278)....
Numerous mounds covering the remains of *Hittite* and
other towns attest its former settlement and cultivation.
This district is full of artificial mounds, some of great size,
that await the spade of the explorer."

We make these quotations to show that this district
south of the road to Aintab was anciently inhabited by
the *Hittites*, which confirms our placing of this boundary;
as is said in Joshua (Chapter 1: 4): "*All the land of the
Hittites*, and unto the Great Sea shall be your boundary."
Taking this with what we quoted above of Ezekiel's description—about the border passing across the territories
of ancient Hamath and Aleppo (Beroea) —we are fully
justified in locating the border so as to include the ancient
Hittite habitations.

HAZAR ENAN (AINTAB)

Passing the valley of the Afrîn (Ziphron) our text
directs us, for the termination of the northern border,
to *Hazar Enan*. This name implies *a village or court of
springs:* and when we turn to examine the site of the ancient
city of *Aintâb*, about three hours distant, we find it answering this description: On the map of "Nord-Syria," in the
Atlas accompanying the work *Reisen in Kleinasien, etc.*,
mentioned above, can be seen the river Ain el-Leben,
whose source is about three miles southwest of Aintâb,

taking its course in a semi-circle toward that city, thence running eastward, passing through the length of the city. (This river is also described in said work, pp. 117, 171.) No less than seven streams from as many different fountains, in the west and northwest, fall into this river at different places between its bend and the city, all of which are carried in and through the city. In addition to these there are three other springs near by, one northward and two eastward which unite and flow into the Ain el-Leben after its exit from Aintâb. The same work also mentions in the "Details of Route" (from Tell Duluk to Aintab) the following: "Am Wege ein Felsbrunnen; weiterhin an mehreren Brunnenhäusern vorüber." Tell Duluk is about four minutes northwest of Aintab and in this interval the "Rock-Well" was met first and the "Well-houses" further on, nearer *Aintab*. Also to be mentioned is the "Good Spring," at *Sam*, in which are sacred fish, two hours from Aintâb, as reported by General Wilson, previously quoted.

Thus we see that *Aintâb* is surrounded by so many springs and fountains, most of them flowing into the city, that the name *Hazar Enan*, the village or court of Springs, well fitted it and had been applied to it in Biblical times; but the Arameans called it "Aintâb" which has about the same meaning in their own language. We, therefore, have good reasons for the identification of *Hazar Enan* with *Aintâb*, which marks the northeastern corner of the promised land.

CHAPTER VI

THE EASTERN BOUNDARY

"AND you shall turn yourselves to the eastern border, from Hazar Enan to Shepham; and the boundary shall go down from Shepham to Riblah, to the eastward of Ayin; and the boundary shall descend and shall touch upon the coast of the Sea of Chinnereth, eastward; and the border shall go down to the Jordan, and terminate at the Salt Sea." (Numbers XXXIV: 10, 11, 12.)

Of the five landmarks given here for the direction of the eastern boundary, the last three were always known and never doubted; but the first two, Shepham and Riblah, disappeared from the records of travelers for many centuries and their location became unknown until about the middle of the last century.

With reference to Shepham, which is Apamea (as translated by both Targums, Jonathan and Jerushalmi, Numbers XXXIV: 7), Dr. Robinson says (*Later Bibl. Res.* Vol. III, page 550): "Apamea of Syria lay upon the hills east of the lower valley of the Orontes. It was a city of importance, and continued to be a strong place during the centuries of the crusades. Abulfeda speaks of it as Famieh or Afamieh (in this last form it is mentioned in the Mishnah, Tract. Hallah IV, 11). But the name has been forgotten in those regions, having been superseded by that of a modern castle near the site, *Kulat el-Mudik*.... Thomson in 1846 was the first to discover and describe the extensive ruins.... They lie just east and northeast of the castle, about three hundred feet above the valley of the Orontes."

Of Riblah, the same author says (ib. page 544): "No one, I believe, questions the identity of Ribleh with the ancient *Riblah* of the Old Testament." On the following page (545) the author reminds us of the encampments at ·Riblah by the kings of Egypt and Babylon (and their cruelties) at or near the time of the destruction of the first temple, as related in 2 Kings (XXIII: 31; XXIV: 25), and by Jeremiah (LII: 9, 10). And he further says: "Under the circumstances, a more advantageous place of encampment for the hosts of Egypt and Babylon can hardly be imagined. On the banks of a mountain stream, in the midst of this vast and fertile plain, the most abundant supplies of provisions and forage were at hand......Riblah indeed disappeared from history and is no more heard of until the present (the nineteenth) century......while Apamea has sunk into oblivion under its present name of Kulat el-Mudik......In the year 1816 Buckingham, passing from Baalbek to Hums, found Ribleh 'as a small cluster of houses' at the elbow of the Orontes. He seems not to have recognized its antiquity; but its identity with the ancient Riblah was soon pointed out by Gesenius. It was visited by Thomson in 1846; and several others passed through it."

Our author further says (ib.): "The absence of all mention of Riblah in the ancient ecclesiastical Notice, shows that it was not a place of importance in the early centuries of Christianity. Nor does its name appear in the records of the long ages from that time to the present century."

This is really a mystery. The antiquity of Riblah, especially its being designated as a landmark of the boundary, could not well have escaped mention in the records of travelers during so many centuries. But we notice an incidence which may solve the question, namely, we find that both Targums, Jonathan and Jerushalmi, render this Riblah of our text, "Daphne." So does R. Saadye Gaon (892–942), in his Arabic translation of the Pentateuch render this Riblah, "Daphne" (J. Schwarz, *"Descriptive Geogr. of Palestine,"* Phil. 1850) whence it may be supposed that Riblah like Apamea, for some reason had also undergone a change of name. The reason suggests itself by the fact mentioned that Riblah was so well suited for the encampment of kings with their hosts; and, as Robinson says (ib.) "The great plain of the Orontes continued to be the storehouse and battlefield of conflicting hosts during the long dominion of the Syro-Macedonian kings, the Romans, etc." It may readily be imagined that a place of this kind must have had suitable buildings for the accommodation of the potentates, their generals, their retinue, and their subordinates. These personages, it will be admitted, would not refrain from indulging in their wonted pleasures and their lustful habits, *while waiting*, and in time the place was probably fitted up for this purpose with beautiful groves and pavilions, statues and altars in and around which idolatrous festivities took place, for which the name "Daphne" was adopted — an expressive name for similar places elsewhere.

This name instead of Riblah was brought home by travelers or pilgrims during the many centuries; but the former name *Riblah* was left, as a tradition, on the lips of the immediate inhabitants, as related by the discoverers, "that their guides and all others told them that this place is the ancient Riblah"; and since then "no one," as Robinson says, "doubts its identity." Thus may be explained the disappearance of Riblah from the outside world, and also, why we find it called "Daphne."

The text of Numbers XXXIV above quoted says: "And the boundary shall go down from Shepham to Riblah, to the eastward of Ayin." For the better understanding of this designation the statement of Major C. R. Conder may be quoted (*Palestine*, p. 192): "The true source of the Orontes is found west of Baalbek, but the main supply of water is from the spring nearly thirty miles farther north, now called 'Ain el Asy.'" Thirty miles north from west of Baalbek is a point a short distance south of Riblah, where the spring is located; and the border passed east of that spring. Dr. Robinson has shown the location of the spring more definitely (*Later Bibl. Res.*, Vol. III, p. 538): "the main fountain is at a point twenty or thirty yards east of the junction with the Nahr Lebweh." Hence, the text "from Shepham to Riblah to the eastward of Ayin" (the fountain or spring).

Having now fairly established all the landmarks of the eastern boundary of the Holy Land, we are enabled to draw the border line from the northeastern to the southeastern corners, i. e. from Hazar Enan (Aintâb) to the southeast corner of the Salt Sea; touching, by the way, all the landmarks designated.

On the whole, we behold the shape of the Promised Land as a rectangle (in a general way), agreeing with the requirements of our text in delineating the borders on the south, west, north and east sides, respectively.

SUPPLEMENT

TO

THE TRUE BOUNDARIES
OF THE HOLY LAND

SUPPLEMENT

CHAPTER I

SCRIPTURAL ALLOTMENTS—PROVISIONAL GRANTS

THE object of this treatise is to explain the description given of the territory allotted to the Israelites for their inheritance, as designated in Numbers XXXIV: 1–12, which became, in the lapse of time, unintelligible and which late discoveries now make it possible to illustrate.

In treating this subject it should be mentioned that there are other Scriptural passages referring to the allotment, in which the territory is extended beyond that designated in the above text of Numbers wherein the Jordan bounds the east, and Kadesh Barnea and the *brook* of Egypt, the south. The different passages occur as follows:

SCRIPTURAL ALLOTMENTS

(1) "Unto thy seed have I given this land, from the river of Egypt (the Nile) unto the great river, the river Euphrates." (Genesis XV: 18–20.)

This is the original promise made to Abraham. It will be noted that the *river of Egypt* is far west of the *brook of Egypt*, and the *Euphrates* is far east of the *Jordan*.

(2) "And I will set thy bounds from the Red Sea unto the sea of the Philistines, and from the desert unto the river." (Exodus XXIII: 31.)

That only additional extensions are mentioned here is evidently because the main land was already designated in the context (v. 23). These, together, agree in substance with the original grant, and were again promised to the Israelites on their acceptance of the *provisory* covenant at Mount Sinai.

(3) Next in order comes our text of Numbers in which the territory is circumscribed —not extended to the Euphrates in the east, nor to the Red Sea or the Nile in the south. (Numbers XXXIV: 1–12.)

We have still two more passages on the subject: (4) "From the desert and the Lebanon, from the river, the river Euphrates, even unto the Western Sea shall be your boundary." (Deuteronomy XI: 24.)

(5) "From the desert and this Lebanon even unto the great river, the river Euphrates, all the land of the Hittites, and unto the Great Sea......shall be your boundary." (Joshua I: 4.)

These apparently discrepant allotments may be explained as follows:

The promise made to Abram was kept in its full extent to his descendants, but when they made and worshipped the golden calf, *whereby they broke the principal condition on which the covenant and all promises were based, they forfeited all privileges.* Following Moses' intercession and their own repentance (Exodus XXXIV: 4), they were restored but not to the same degree as before; hence, the first two passages quoted above and our text of Numbers do not clash nor contradict; the latter is indeed a *reduced* grant.

The last two passages quoted also come in line. They are nothing less than kind exhortation, informing the people of a great and good principle, viz: that God's conditional promises of good, though they be (for just cause) withheld or abridged for a time, yet are never abrogated, but are reserved for fulfillment as soon as the provisos or conditions be observed; as it is said (Deuteronomy VII: 9), "Know then that the Eternal thy God is the faithful

God, who keepeth the covenant and the kindness for those that love Him and keep His commandments to the thousandth generation."

PROVISIONAL GRANTS

By carefully perusing the contexts of these two passages, the attentive reader may almost hear the kindly exhortation ringing in his ear, proclaiming: "For, if ye will but keep all this commandment which I command you to do it......Then will the Eternal drive out all these nations from before you......Every place whereon the sole of your foot may tread shall be yours; from the wilderness and the Lebanon, from the river Euphrates, even unto the Western Sea shall be your boundary" (Deuteronomy XI: 22–24). This refers to the fulfillment of the original promise: "From the wilderness (of Sinai) and Lebanon," i. e. from south to north; "from the Euphrates to the Sea" is from east to west, in both of which are included the granted extensions.

Likewise does the passage in Joshua (I: 4) refer to the entire promise with the proviso in its context (v. 7) "Only be thou strong and very courageous to observe to do according to all the law which Moses, My servant, hath commanded thee," etc.

Accordingly, the gift in the first two passages relates to what might have been; in the last two, to what will be (at some future time). These are not, however, the subjects of our present discussion. We will concern ourselves only with the third one (Numbers XXXIV: 1–12) wherein the territory is as minutely circumscribed as in a modern deed, the main part of which was actually conquered and taken possession of, as was foretold.

To locate correctly this inheritance to which Israel hopes to be gloriously restored, as assured by a host of prophets, is our aim and purpose.

CHAPTER II

CAUSES OF MISINTERPRETATION—CHANGE OF GEOGRAPHICAL NAMES

HAVING explained the different Scriptural passages relating to the extent of the Promised Land and shown that they do not contradict one another, we shall now proceed to discuss and examine the causes which led to the misconception of the text of Numbers (XXXIV: 1–12), wherein the boundaries on all sides are described, but which at present is not correctly interpreted. Its vagueness may be judged by the widely different opinions of its expositors.

The origin of this divergence of opinion lies mainly in the change of the *geographical names* (as mentioned in the Introduction), and also in other causes, chief among which was Ptolemy's *Geography*. His 'Map of Palestine and part of Syria' has been published among others by the New York Geographical Society, also in Major Conder's *Palestine*, page 2. Ptolemy, the great astronomer who wrote the well known *Almagest*, was also a celebrated geographer. Chambers' Encyclopedia writes of him: "The 'Almagest' and the 'Geography' were *the standard text-books to succeeding ages;* the first, till the time of Copernicus, the second, till the great maritime discoveries of the 15th century showed its deficiencies." (See Map I.)

The map above referred to was a part of these geographical standard texts. On this map are the two mighty ridges, Lebanon and Anti-Lebanon, *misplaced* so far (east) beyond the limits of Palestine that they could not be included within its borders, and the large tract covered by the *real* Lebanons, not having been known as such, must have been considered foreign territory and therefore could not be included within said boundaries[1]; consequently, the northern border, to conform with Ptolemy's text, had to be drawn *south* of the real Lebanons, which is the north of Joshua's conquest.[2]

Another important reason for the misunderstanding of our text in Numbers is this, that it became the general belief, that the Holy Land as conquered and divided among the Tribes (by Joshua) was also the Promised Land allotted in Numbers (XXXIV: 1–12), and that the Promised Land and the Conquered Land had the same extension and the same borders. Therefore Mount Hor was identified with Mount Hermon (*Palestine*, H. S. Osborn, Philadelphia, 1859, p. 571; Map of Ancient Palestine, *Univ. Pron. Dictionary*, Thomas Wright, London and New York, about same date; Mount Hor marked on Anti-Lebanon).

---

[1] To further describe how the Lebanons are misplaced on that map, it may be said, that these two ridges which really have their southern beginnings at the north of Joshua's conquests (from Baal-Gad in the east unto Zidon [Saida] in the west) and thence run northward, are so subverted as to have their northern beginnings at a point about fifty-seven statute miles due east of Baalbek, thence running in a *southeasterly* direction into the great Syrian desert; and that of Anti-Lebanon about fifty miles east of the southern end of the *real* Anti-Lebanon, thence extending parallel with his Lebanon into the same desert (see Map 1). In such a situation, no one, not even Ptolemy himself, would include these Lebanons within the Promised Land.

[2] However, Maundrell in 1697 (*Journey from Aleppo to Jerusalem*, p. 482 f), and Adrianus Relandus (*Palæstina Monumentis veteribus illustrata*, ed. 1714, I, 311 ff) already knew the real situation and extension of the Lebanon and Anti-Lebanon.

CHAPTER III

THE LEBANONS—BIBLICAL PASSAGES

THE many Scriptural passages relating to the Lebanons show that the true situation of these mountains was well known to the authors, and help us in an indirect way to understand our passage in Numbers XXXIV and the northern border.

As to the Anti-Lebanon we read in Joshua (XIII: 1–5): "Now Joshua was old, well stricken in years, and the Lord said unto him, Thou art old, stricken in years, and of the land there *remaineth yet very much* to be taken possession of. This is the land that yet remaineth: All the boundaries of the Philistines, and of all Geshuri, and Me'arah of the Zidonians up to *Apheka*" (which is Afka[1] on the way from Zidon to the Cedars of Lebanon). "And the land of the Giblites, and *all Lebanon*, toward the rising of the sun (the eastern Lebanon) from Baal-Gad under Mount Hermon up to the entrance of Hamath." This plainly indicates that Mount Hermon is the southern beginning of the eastern Lebanon and that the eastern Lebanon thence runs northward to the "entrance of Hamath" which is, therefore, in the north of the Lebanon. Hamath is the name of a very ancient city and of its territory in northern Syria and it is also one of the landmarks of the northern border of our text (Numbers XXXIV) which will be treated in its proper place.

The continuation of the passage in Joshua XIII just quoted speaks about the Western Lebanon. In v. 6 we read: "All the inhabitants of the mountain from Lebanon unto Misrephoth-Mayim (Sarepta, Surafend,) all the Zidonians (Saida); these will I drive out, etc." There can be no doubt that this verse refers to the western Lebanon

---

[1]See Robinson, *Later Bib. Res.*, Volume 3, pp. 603–608. Boston, 1857.

running northward along the Great Sea coast passing by Sarepta and Saida at its southern end. Farther north we find this ridge in connection with the memorable cedars cut from Lebanon by Hiram, king of Tyre, for the building of King Solomon's temple. In his message to Hiram, King Solomon says: "And now command thou that they (his servants) hew me cedar trees out of Lebanon" (1 Kings V: 20).[1] And in his answer, Hiram says: "My servants shall bring them down from the Lebanon unto the sea" (V: 23).[1] This is repeated in substance in 2 Chronicles (II: 7–15). Our text mentions *no* transportation but simply "the bringing them down from the Lebanon to the sea" which implies their proximity.

Thus we see that the Biblical description of the situation of the Lebanons is fully corroborated by the geographical facts and the error is purely on the side of Ptolemy. Howbeit, we are not responsible for Ptolemy's errors. His map of Palestine was here introduced to show one cause for the erroneous popular belief in vogue for nearly two thousand years, viz: that the northern boundary of the Promised Land designated in Numbers XXXIV, coincided with the northern boundary of Joshua's conquest. But the geographical explorations have scattered to the winds all these former conceptions and have established the fact that the Lebanons are a northern continuation of the territory conquered by Joshua, as was known to all ancient Biblical students from the texts of Joshua and Kings above cited.

The Lebanons Within the Boundaries of the Promised Land

From these very citations, we can learn not only the true location of the Lebanons but also, that they were included within the boundaries of Numbers XXXIV. Joshua was told (Joshua XIII: 1): "And of the land

---

[1] Verses are numbered according to original Hebrew text. (American Revised Version, 1 Kings V: 6, 9).

there *remaineth* yet very much to be conquered." The definite expression *"the* land" no doubt refers to the land promised to Israel as described in Numbers XXXIV, because it was this allotment which was Joshua's task to conquer, and as the Lebanons are included in the list of the remaining lands (v. 5, 6), it is plain that they were included within that allotment — remaining unconquered.

Another proof, equally sufficient, can be deduced from what is narrated in Judges (I: 27–35; II: 1–3), where the Israelites are rebuked for not destroying all the nations with their idolatry from among their newly acquired possessions. This proved to be a snare to the Israelites first by inter-marriage and finally by worshipping their idols (Judges III: 5–6). For this grave offense a divine message came to them saying (Judges II: 20, 21): "For the cause that this people have transgressed My covenant.... verily I will no more drive before them any one of *the nations which Joshua left when he died.*"

Evidently "the nations which Joshua left" must have been those whose territory was included within his task to conquer; and as these nations and their territories, *including Lebanon*, are recounted here (Judges III: 3), it is plain again that the Lebanons were included in the allotment of Numbers.

Another proof may be added from the prayer of Moses (Deuteronomy III: 25): "Let me now pass over (the Jordan), that I may see the goodly land *and the Lebanon.*" Why would Moses desire to see the Lebanon if it were not included in the allotment just made?

Accordingly, the northern boundary of the Promised Land as given in our text must be drawn *north* of the Lebanons. This is, in our opinion, a settled point. But the question yet remains: How far north is that border located? This is a mooted question, the solution of which lies in the identification of the landmarks indicated in the text for that border-line.

CHAPTER IV

THE NORTHERN BORDER

Various Opinions; Esthori Ha-Parchi;
Rabbi Jos. Schwarz

WE will now proceed to consider the opinions of
the most noted expositors on the text, previously
referred to (Chapter II, p. 26) and show that none of
them can be accepted.

Among these various theories as to the designations of
the northern border (Numbers XXXIV: 7, 8, 9) may be
counted:

Prevailing Opinion

(1) The prevailing opinion mentioned in the previous
chapter, (p. 63) viz: the northern border of the text co-
incides with the northern border of Joshua's conquest, i. e.
from "Baal-Gad in the Bukeia of Lebanon" (Joshua
XII: 7) in the east, "to (great) Zidon" (ib. XI: 8, XIX: 28)
in the west; identifying *Mount Hor* with *Mount Hermon*
and the *"entrance of Hamath"* with the *Bukeia* between
the Lebanons. (See Map II.)

(a) This opinion, besides being contradicted by the
several other passages quoted in the previous chapter
(pp. 62 ff) is also inconsistent with its own text which
designates *Mount Hor* as the *first* landmark starting from
the Great Sea eastward, and mentions four more landmarks
before the eastern end is reached. *Mount Hermon* is
situated on the eastern *end* of the land and the borderline
would thus have to pass over the whole width of the land
at random, before it would meet the *first* landmark and
what use then can be made of the other landmarks? Furthermore according to this opinion, the *second* landmark,

5

the "entrance of Hamath," (which is identified with the "Bukeia") must be crossed before the first one is reached, a distortion which cannot be tolerated.

(b)   The *Tosefta* quoted above (pp. 36, 37) in reference to the Great Sea as the western border, says: "The islets in the sea are determined by an imaginary line drawn from Mount Amanon (Mount Hor) to the brook of Egypt; (the islets) inside that line, are included, outside thereof are excluded." This can be said only when the two points touch the sea shore and the sea extends eastward between these points so that the line drawn lies wholly in the sea. But Mount Hermon is over twenty miles away from the sea; the line drawn from it would have to cross diagonally the whole width of the land before it would reach the sea, (see Map II) and therefore would not serve that purpose: Mount Hermon cannot be Mount Hor.

ESTHORI HA-PARCHI

(2)   The second opinion (in order of time) was that of Esthori Ha-Parchi, one of the Jewish exiles of France in 1306, who after visiting Egypt, emigrated to the Holy Land and became a resident of Beth-Shean (Scythopolis). After traveling and making observations throughout the land, he wrote his famous book *Kaftor va-ferach* in 1322 (2nd ed. Edelmann, Berlin, 1852, cf. pp. 42 ff).

Esthori was the first one to protest against the then prevailing belief and to proclaim that Mount Hor is not Mount Hermon; thus, in describing the former mountain, he says, p. 24a; "Hermon, with its other four names (see Deuteronomy III: 9; IV: 48; Cant. IV: 8) has no relation here."

He, also, was the first to recognize and locate the Lebanons in their true situation after they were hidden over a thousand years by Ptolemy's delusive maps. He

identifies *Jebel el-Akra* with *Mount Hor* and says: "All
the land between it and the Brook of Egypt, as Laodicea
(Latakia), Gebal, Tripolis, Beiruth, Zidon, Tyre, etc., is
according to the text, within the boundaries; and the
Scripture which recounts the land of the Canaanite and
the Lebanon (Deuteronomy I: 7) among the promised
possessions, alludes to this Lebanon country." No one
at that time ventured such declarations. (See Map III.)

But, in locating the boundaries he was not so successful.
From *Jebel el-Akra* (his Mount Hor), near Râs el-Basît,
between Ladikîyeh and Alexandretta, he draws the line
southeast to Hamath which he adopts as the second
landmark; thence he turns the line southwest to a place
"about a day's journey from Hamath" which he calls
Hazan el-Akrat, the modern Hosn el-Akrâd (Robinson, *Later
Bibl. Researches*, Vol. 3, pp. 557, 565). Esthori Ha-Parchi
identifies this place with the biblical Hazar Enan, mentioned in our text (Numbers XXXIV: 9) as the eastern
end of the border and the northeastern corner of the
Promised Land. Thence he draws the eastern border in
a south south-westerly direction to *Dan* (Laish) which he
identifies with Shepham[1] of our text (Numbers XXXIV:
10, 11); thence to the eastern shore of Gennesareth and
the Jordan, to the southern end of the Salt Sea. *Ziphron*
is left unknown, and of *Riblah* of our text he says: "It
appears that this is not the same Riblah mentioned in
Jeremiah" (LII: 9) but he does not locate it.

This opinion, though an improvement on the old prevailing one, does not at all agree with the directions of
our text for the following reasons:

---

[1]The reason for this identification seems to be as follows: Our text says:
"And ye shall turn yourselves to the eastern border from Hazar Enan to
Shepham" (Numbers XXXIV: 10). Shepham then is the next landmark
on the eastern border south after Hazar Enan, and as the next landmark
he met south of his Hazar Enan was Dan (Laish), he concluded than Dan
(Laish) must be another name for Shepham.

(a) Our text directs the northern boundary to pass through five landmarks from west to east; whereas according to his theory the northern boundary has no extent but is the point of an acute angle (see Map III).

(b) The line running from *Jebel el-Akra* to *Hamath* shows more correctly an *eastern* than a *northern* boundary; it is out of all reason to go back in a *southwesterly* direction from Hamath to Hosn el-Akrâd to find a *northeastern* corner which Hazar Enan should be. This is sufficient for the rejection of his *Hazar Enan*.

(c) The identification of Dan (Laish) with *Shepham* is simply absurd, depending on the erroneous identity of his Hazar Enan as a premise. However, the late discovery of *Apamea*[1] and its identification with Shepham[2] settles this matter without dispute. This theory, also, must be rejected.

Rabbi Joseph Schwarz

(3) Since Esthori's time no other discussion of note appeared until the middle of the last century, when a third opinion was advanced by Rabbi Joseph Schwarz, a native of Bavaria, Germany. After having received a thorough education in the Hebrew literature and a collegiate course at home, he emigrated to Palestine, which he desired to explore. He settled in Jerusalem and carried on his ideal work for many years, which resulted in publishing his *Descriptive Geography of Palestine*, (an English translation of his original work in rabbinic Hebrew; Philadelphia, 1850), in which he delineated the boundaries differently.

Although he had succeeded in making many valuable discoveries and his book is replete with new interesting finds, his delineation of the boundaries, nevertheless, is, as that of his predecessors, erroneous.

---

[1] Robinson, *Later Bibl. Res.* p. 550; Boston 1857.

[2] Targums Jonathan and Jerushalmi; Ch. VI; Suppl., pp. 74, 76.

His western border line, which runs on the coast of the Great Sea northward ends at Jebel Nuriyah, a peak on Râs Shakka, south of Tripolis, in thirty-four degrees twenty minutes N. L., which he identifies with Mount Hor. Then (in his own language, pp. 29, 30), "eastward through the great valley of Coelesyria (his entrance to Hamath) towards *Al Djededa*, east of Tripolis (which he takes for Zedad, p. 26); then somewhat southeasterly through the mountain of *Sefira* (his Ziphron); from there to the village *Dar Kanon* (his Hazar Enan); then, southerly to the village *Banias*, over the *western* shore of the sea Semechonitis (Bahr el-Huleh, where he locates Riblah), to the Jordan." (See Map IV.)

This theory, it seems, is an improvement on the preceding one in so far that at least a part of its northern outline resembles a northern border (in taking an easterly direction), and that Ziphron and Riblah of our text are located. But, on the whole, this outline cannot be entertained for the following reasons:

(a) Our text which says: "*From* the Great Sea shall ye *mark out* for you (the boundary *to*) *Mount Hor*" (ib. v. 7) infers that these two points are two landmarks with some distance between them, just as the next mark (v. 8) which is similarly phrased in the original. Therefore, "Râs Shakka," being a promontory closely connected with the sea, cannot be Mount Hor.

(b) The line drawn from that mountain across Lebanon to Coelesyria is highly improbable as a boundary-line. It would run a little south of the great cedars, concerning which Dr. Robinson (*Later Bibl. Res.*, Vol. 3, pp. 586–90) describes the difficulty of even a bridle passage. He reached the vale of the cedars, sixty-four hundred feet above sea level, yet, "The peaks of Lebanon above rise nearly three thousand feet higher" (*ibid.* p. 591). This objection may also be applied to the preceding theory of Esthori.

(c)   The same anomaly noticed in the preceding theory exists here also; on looking at Map IV, which is copied from his book, it will be seen that his outline from Jebel Nuriyah to his Hazar Enan is composed of three broken lines resembling three sides of a square and these are given to constitute the northern boundary.   And his Hazar Enan, which should be a northeastern corner, is not in the north and is not a corner.[1]

Again, he, like Esthori, identifies Shepham with Dan (Laish), which is incorrect.   Furthermore, he rejects the true Riblah on the eastern border (Numbers XXXIV: 12), and substitutes for it Daphne on the west of Lake Huleh: for the reason that the true Riblah is rendered in the Targums by *Daphne* (see Chapter VI page 50), and that there were two Riblahs.   But the fact that Riblah is called Daphne in the Targums, is no reason why all "Daphnes" should be Riblah.   There were several Daphnes throughout the land but only one "Riblah, in the land of Hamath" (2 Kings XXIII: 35 a. o.).   Besides this the existence of a Daphne on the west of Lake Huleh is very uncertain.[2]

Finally, in order to extend the border line to his Riblah, he had to draw it to the west of Lake Huleh, thus excluding that lake and vicinity (Joshua's last and greatest conquest) from within the boundary; and then turn the border again eastward, crossing the Jordan between this lake and the Sea of Gennesareth in order to touch upon the eastern shoulder of that sea as directed by our text (Numbers XXXIV: 11).

All these conclusions are unwarranted.   With all due appreciation for the learning and piety of these two rabbins their opinions of the boundaries cannot be accepted.

---

[1] Thinking his outline might show a better figure when his points are placed on the correct maps, we have tried it (see Map III) but the result shows no improvement.

[2] Why the true Riblah was called Daphne can be seen on page 52.

CHAPTER V

THE THEORY OF ROBINSON AND PORTER

THERE is one more theory that is entitled to consideration as it emanates from and is advocated by many of the best modern explorers:—Drs. Robinson, Porter and others (see p. 26).

The fundamental part of this theory is based on the landmark "the entering in of Hamath" mentioned in our text (Numbers XXXIV: 8) on the northern border, their identification of which, they supposed, was clear and conclusive. This entrance, they say, is the pass from the sea-shore between the northern end of Lebanon and the Bargylus mountains in the north, where a valley of some extent carrying the Nahr el-Kebîr, (the Eleutherus river of antiquity,) to the sea intersects these mountains. (See Map V.) This pass, Porter says, "is the natural entrance of Hamath from the Mediterranean." This, "I conceive to be identical with the way of Hethlon in Ezekiel. This way of Hethlon is said to be 'as men go to Zedad' in one place; while in another it is said to be 'as men go to Hamath.' Both descriptions are correct; for the pass above referred to, is the natural and indeed the only entrance to Zedad, the present Sudad, and to Hamath" (Porter, *Five years in Damascus*, Vol. II, p. 356). The passages in Ezekiel alluded to are Ezekiel XLVII: 15 and XLVIII: 1.

"We may conclude," writes Porter, "that the Great Mountain referred to is the northern and loftiest part of Libanus."

"The border therefore ran from the shore of the Mediterranean across the level tract of the coast toward

71

the northern brow of this range and then swept through the great pass to the border of the plain on the east." (ib. p. 357.)

Robinson says: "*The entering in of Hamath*......The Mediterranean being the western border, the northern border was to run from the sea to 'Mount Hor'; thence 'unto the entrance of Hamath' and thence to Zedad now Sudad......All these notices show clearly that 'the entering in of Hamath' was at the northern extremity of Lebanon......between the northern end of Lebanon and the Nusairiyeh mountains. Mount Hor was obviously between the sea shore and the Bukeia." (*Later Biblical Researches*, Volume III, pp. 568, 569).

The same author says: "No one I believe questions the identity of *Riblah* with the ancient *Ribleh* of the old Testament. It is first mentioned as on the northern part of the eastern border of the Promised Land; which border was to pass from Shepham by Riblah and so down through the Bukeia and Wady et-Teim to the lake of Chinnereth" (ib. p. 544).

Thus we see that they both agree as to the identification of Mount Hor and also as to "the entering in of Hamath" that it is the great pass between the northern end of Lebanon and the southern end of the Nosairiyeh mountains (the Mons Bargylus of the ancients), running to the great plain on the east. But further on, their opinions differ; Robinson draws the line thence to Sadad, but Porter marks the border as follows:

"The boundary line must have gone near the city (of Hamath)......The border would run from the opening in the mountains northeast to Hamath. The goings forth of the border are said to be to Zedad and also to Hazar Enan......The site of the former is known; but where is the latter?......There is, in fact, only one spot in this whole region that would seem to answer to the description, and that is Kuryetein, where there are large fountains, etc." (ib. p. 357, 358.)

The eastern border differs, as Porter thinks, in Ezekiel and Numbers. "Ezekiel extended the eastern border much farther than Moses. The latter brings it from Hazar Enan, which appears to have been at or near the northern extremity, to Riblah. We know nothing of Shepham, which was situated between these two places, but it *lay probably to the south of Sudad*. This line there-fore......would sweep round, with a curve to the south, from Kuryetein to Riblah, and there turn southward along the western base of Antilibanus and Hermon, to the sea of Tiberias. The plain of Hums would thus be included, together with the Bukeia, but the whole territory of Damascus left out. In Ezekiel, Damascus is included with the country east of the Jordan." (ib. p. 359.)

This, is in summary, the description of the boundaries of the Holy Land as given in Scripture (Numbers XXXIV: 3–12), according to the opinion, partly of Robinson, but mainly of Porter; but, with due regard for their wisdom, we must say that it is unacceptable.

On glancing at Map V, it will be seen that the bor-der line running from Hamath to Sadad runs from north to south with but a small inclination toward the east so that it would be more proper to call it the *eastern* than include it in the *northern* border; Hamath then would be more properly the northeastern corner than Karyatein, which is not in the north and is not a corner, but a small eastern projection. The "curve" is not mentioned in Scripture, but is Porter's own invention in order to have the line pass his Shepham, which he thought was south of Sadad.

Continuing, the line runs from south to north until it reaches Riblah (a distance of over forty miles) in a directly opposite direction to Scriptural description.

Moreover the writer, as seen before, conjectured that Shepham "lay probably to the *south* of Sadad." But the Targums of Jonathan and Jerushalmi render Shepham by *Apamea*. The position of this place, the modern Kalat el-Mudîk (Robinson, *Later Bibl. Res.*, vol. III, p. 550) is about thirty-five degrees thirty minutes North, thirty-six degrees twenty-five minutes East (i. e. about eighty miles *north* of Sadad).[1] The border line, (to conform to Scripture) must therefore be drawn from Karyatein (his Hazar Enan) to Shepham (Apamea), a distance of about ninety miles, running in the *opposite direction*, from south to north (after it has descended from Hamath to Karyatein from north to south about eighty miles) and then return from Shepham to Riblah, north to south again, a distance of about seventy miles. (See Map V.)

This would cause the lines to intersect each other in distorted confusion and would not show which territory is included within nor which territory is excluded from this meshwork.

Zedad cannot be represented by Sadad because according to Numbers (XXXIV: 7–9) Zedad is on the northern border and is obviously *north* and west of Hamath and Riblah while Sadad is *south* and east of them. Much less can Hazar Enan be represented by Karyatein, for the former is the *northeastern* corner of the land, while the latter is even farther *south* than Sadad. These, therefore, cannot be identical.

Porter's concluding statement, as quoted above: "In Ezekiel, Damascus is included (within the eastern boundary) with the country east of the Jordan" is also contrary to that prophet's declaration in reference to the country east

---

[1] This identification of Shepham with Apamea is now generally abandoned, but *only for the reason* that the place is, according to the different theories about the northern boundary, too far to the north. We have proved that this is not the case. (Chap. VI p. 50).

of the Jordan. This prophet in describing the eastern border says (XLVII: 18): "between the land of Gilead and the land of Israel, the Jordan is the boundary," the same as is dictated in Numbers (XXXIV: 12). As regards Damascus, mentioned in the same verse by Ezekiel, it requires explanation and will be the subject of our discussion in the next chapter.

CHAPTER VI

EZEKIEL'S DESCRIPTION

I T may be proper to state here the cause that induced these learned men, as well as those previously mentioned, to suppose that Hazar Enan, the northeastern extremity, should be located as far *south* as Karyatein or Deir Kânûn.

The reason is that in Ezekiel's description of the boundaries it is said twice "Hazar Enan the boundary of Damascus," (XLVII: 17; XLVIII: 1) which seems to indicate that Hazar Enan is somewhere in the vicinity of Damascus.

But these theorists did not stop to consider that this declaration of Ezekiel, if taken as superficially interpreted, would contradict the many verses of Joshua and of Judges above quoted (Supplement, Chapter III, pp. 62 ff.), which prove conclusively that both *Lebanons* were included within the boundary of Numbers (XXXIV) and consequently Hazar Enan, the northeastern extremity, must be located *north of these ridges;* how then could it be "the boundary of Damascus" which is situated at the *southern* end of them —nearly eighty miles away?

The apparent abnormity of the prophet's assertion becomes still greater if we consider the position of Riblah and Apamea, the latter of which is authoritatively identified[1] with the Shepham of our text (Numbers XXXIV) and is about one hundred and thirty-five miles *north* of Damascus; Hazar Enan being still farther north, how can it be "the boundary of Damascus?"

While looking for a solution of this question another

---

[1] Targums Jonathan and Jerushalmi. Robinson, *Later Bibl. Res.* p. 550.

apparent inconsistency presented itself in the context. There Ezekiel says: (XLVII: 15) "And this shall be the boundary of the land: On the *north* side, from the great sea, the road of Hethlon to the coming in of Zedad:

(16) Hamath, Berotha, Sibrayim, *which is between the boundary of Damascus and the boundary of Hamath*......

(17) And the boundary shall be from the sea to Hazar Enan at the *boundary of Damascus*," etc.[1]

Here we have the full length of the northern boundary line from the sea to Hazar Enan with five places mentioned between the two extremities of the line. This line must necessarily run from the west to the east and must be located, as before said, *north* of Shepham —how, then, could any of those five places be between Damascus and Hamath (as in Ezekiel XLVII: 16 just quoted), when Hamath itself is *south* of Shepham and the place or places designated would thus be *still farther south* of it?

These questions must convince the reader that Ezekiel's declarations are misunderstood, and require an explanation that will solve these problems and show no disagreement with Numbers, Joshua, and Judges. We offer the following solution, founded on facts, viz:

(1) "Damascus" is the name applied to that city and is also the name applied to the territory whereof that city is the capital. The same is the case with "Hamath"; Hamath the city, and "the land of Hamath," "Riblah in the land of 'Hamath'" (2 Kings XXIII and elsewhere), though Riblah is about forty-five miles south of Hamath. So are Tripolis and Aleppo and so was Babel (Babylon) the name of the country and the name of the capital city. When such names are mentioned in Scripture, it should be ascertained which is referred to; in our case it is particularly stated; "the *boundary* of Damascus," "the *boundary* of Hamath."

---

[1] The italics are ours.

(2) Syria, under present Turkish rule, is divided into four vilayets and two liwas. "Damascus" which is one of the vilayets is larger than the other three put together. "The vilayet of Damascus comprises all the territory between the Lebanon and the Euphrates —that is all between latitude thirty-one degrees, thirty-six minutes North and longitude thirty-five degrees, forty-one minutes East. The surface is for the most part level," etc. (Chambers' *Enc.*, *s. v.* Damascus). There must be a reason for this unequal division; and the latter part of this quotation gives it; namely, that "the surface is for the most part *level*" and the land therefore is easy of access in all of its parts so that one governor is sufficient to dominate it though it is extensive; but in the mountainous regions where travel and communication necessary to keep the inhabitants in subjection is much more difficult, the vilayets must be more limited in size. This cause being a physical and therefore immutable condition of the country, we may infer that the same arrangement was necessary and existed under the rule of all the ancient monarchs who reigned successively over the country, and that in Ezekiel's time, contemporaneous with the Babylonian dominion, the province of Damascus was likewise extensive. To understand as well as to substantiate Ezekiel's detailed and emphatic declarations of the northern boundary line, we offer the following as not only the probable, but the only possible explanation:

The territory of Damascus extended northward beyond Hazar Enan, on the north of the continuation of Anti-Lebanon and farther, including Aleppo. Alongside, west of it, in the Bukeia, ran the territory of Hamath, to the same distance north so that the direction of the two was nearly parallel. Confirmatory of this theory is that no mention occurs anywhere in Scripture of the existence of any other province in Syria north of Hamath.

By assuming that this arrangement had been in existence at Ezekiel's time, the two provinces, then, were stretched out side by side from *south to north* while the northern boundary which was running (north of the Lebanons) from *west to east* must have cut across the two provinces, and through their western and eastern boundaries until it reached Hazar Enan, which was located, as Ezekiel declares, "at the boundary of Damascus" (ib. v. 17) i. e. at the eastern boundary of the *territory* of Damascus, though very far from that city — just as may be said: "The Niagara Falls are situated at the boundary of New York," though they are about five hundred miles distant from that *city*. This solves the first question.

The second question may also be explained in the same manner; viz: what Ezekiel said: "Sibrayim which is between the boundary of Damascus and the boundary of Hamath" (XLVII: 16), does not refer to these two cities but to their *territories* which extended side by side far in the north, where the northern boundary cut across them and passed Sibrayim which is situated between the two territories.

By this exposition we can understand Ezekiel's assertions not to conflict with any of the other texts but to give additional landmarks for the same border line to those given in *Numbers*. We are not now restricted to locate Hazar Enan or any other northern landmark in the vicinity of the *city* of Damascus, but we can go up any distance northward along the *territory* of Damascus and opposite the northern end of the Great Sea in quest of these places until we find such as can be identified, by authority and good reason, with our textual designations. As we have followed this idea and have been successful in finding all the textual designations, as well as most of Ezekiel's additions, in the localities where they were expected to be found according to our theory (see Map VI), it is clear proof that we have correctly interpreted all the boundaries.

MAPS

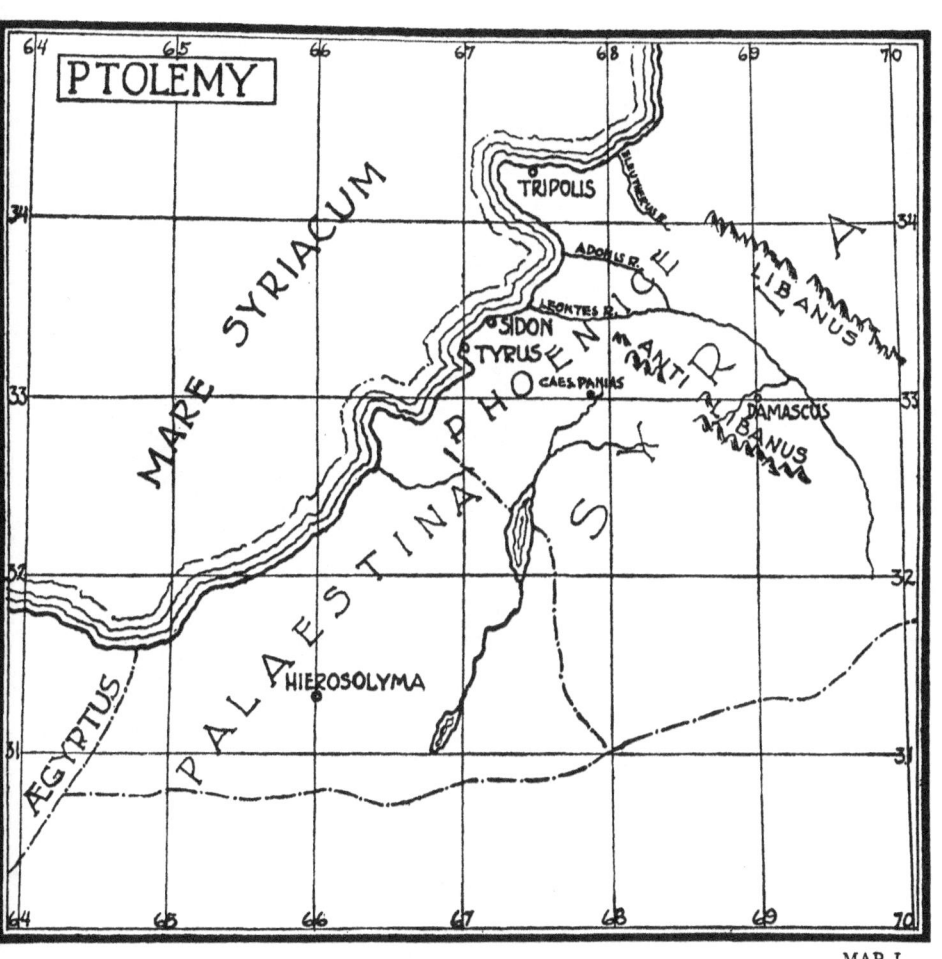

MAP I

Palestine and part of Syria, according to Ptolemy, *c.* 100 A.D
(From *Palestine*, Major C. R. Conder, p. 2)

83

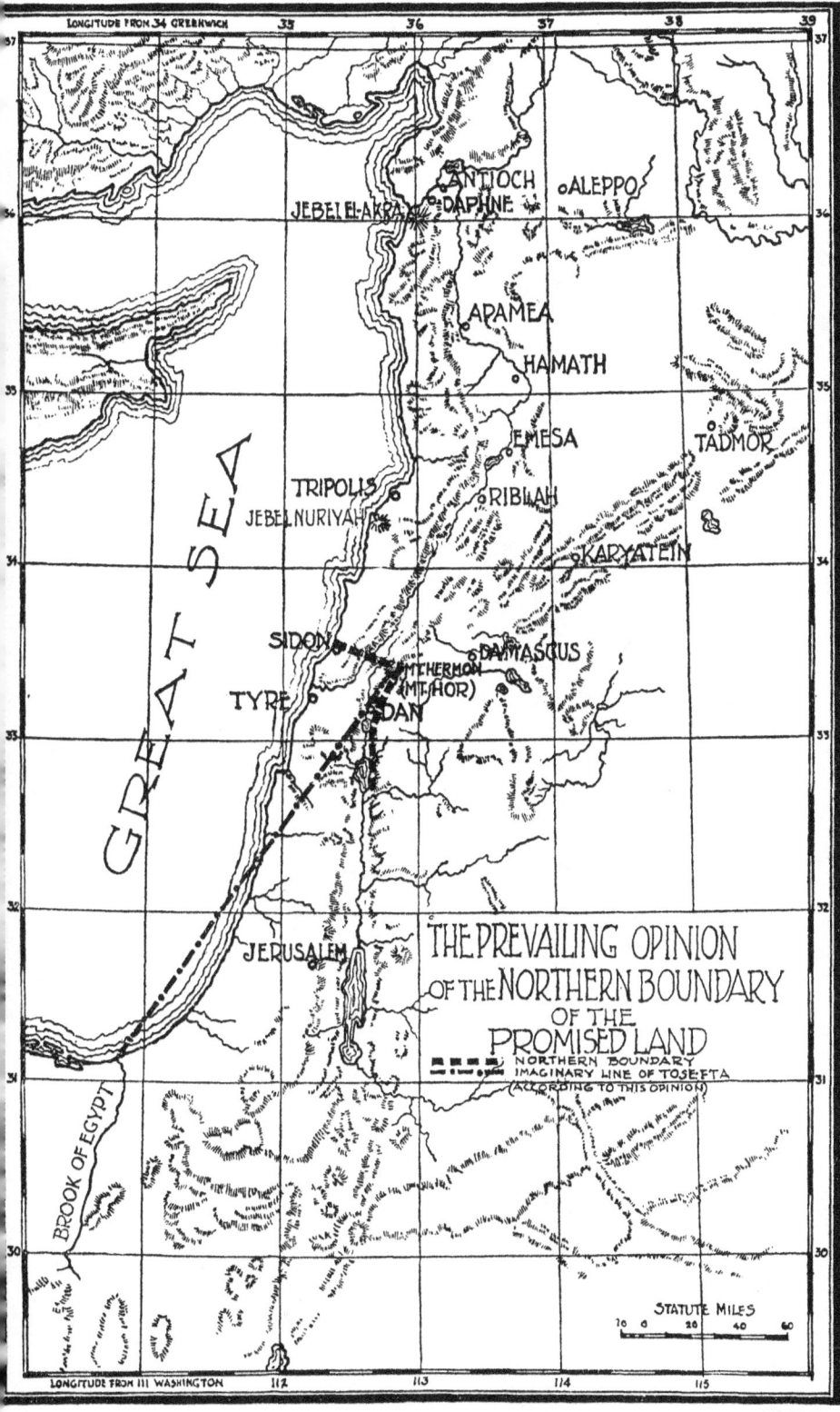

MAP II

85

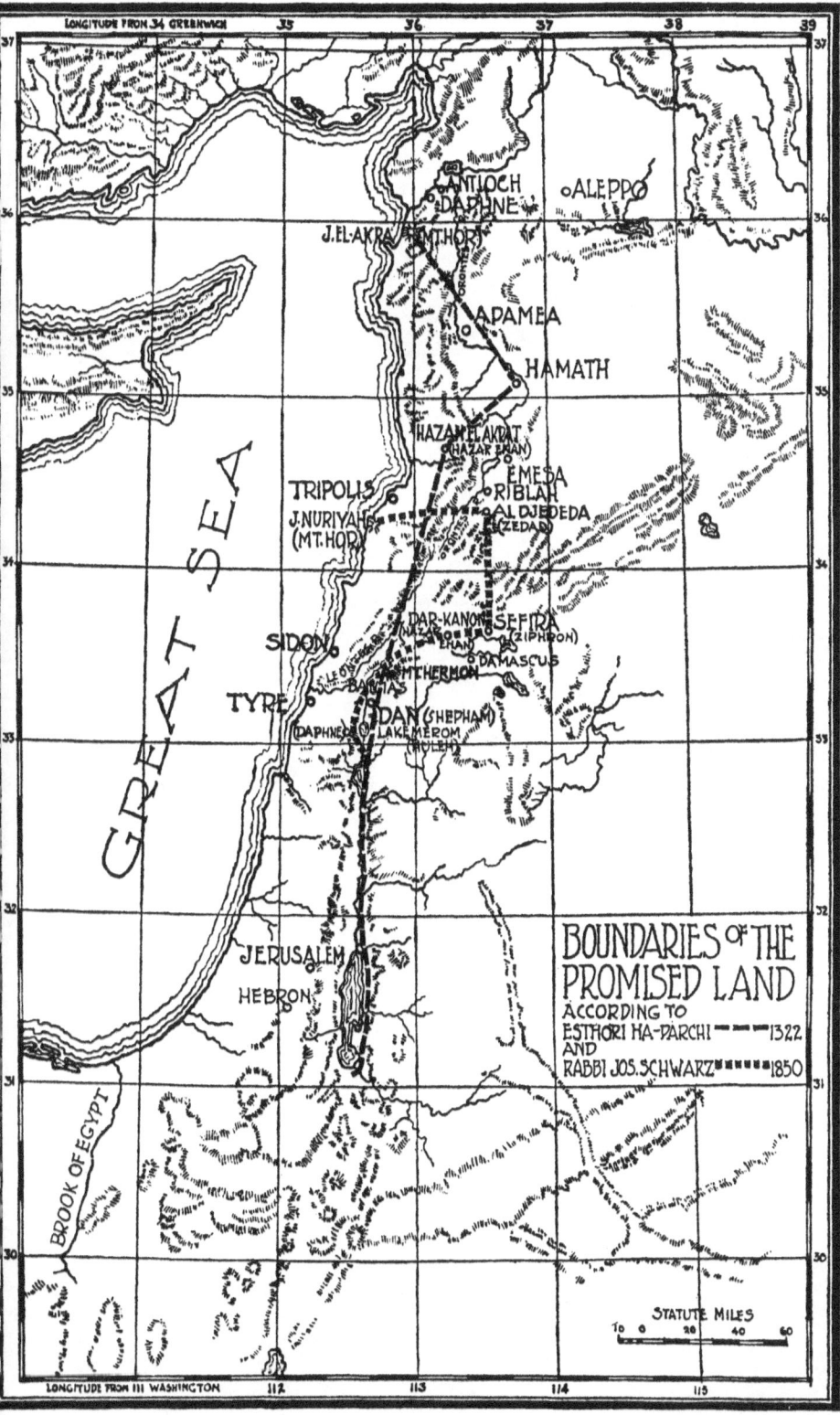

BOUNDARIES OF THE
PROMISED LAND
ACCORDING TO
ESTHORI HA-PARCHI ━━━ 1322
AND
RABBI JOS. SCHWARZ ▪▪▪▪▪ 1850

STATUTE MILES

MAP III

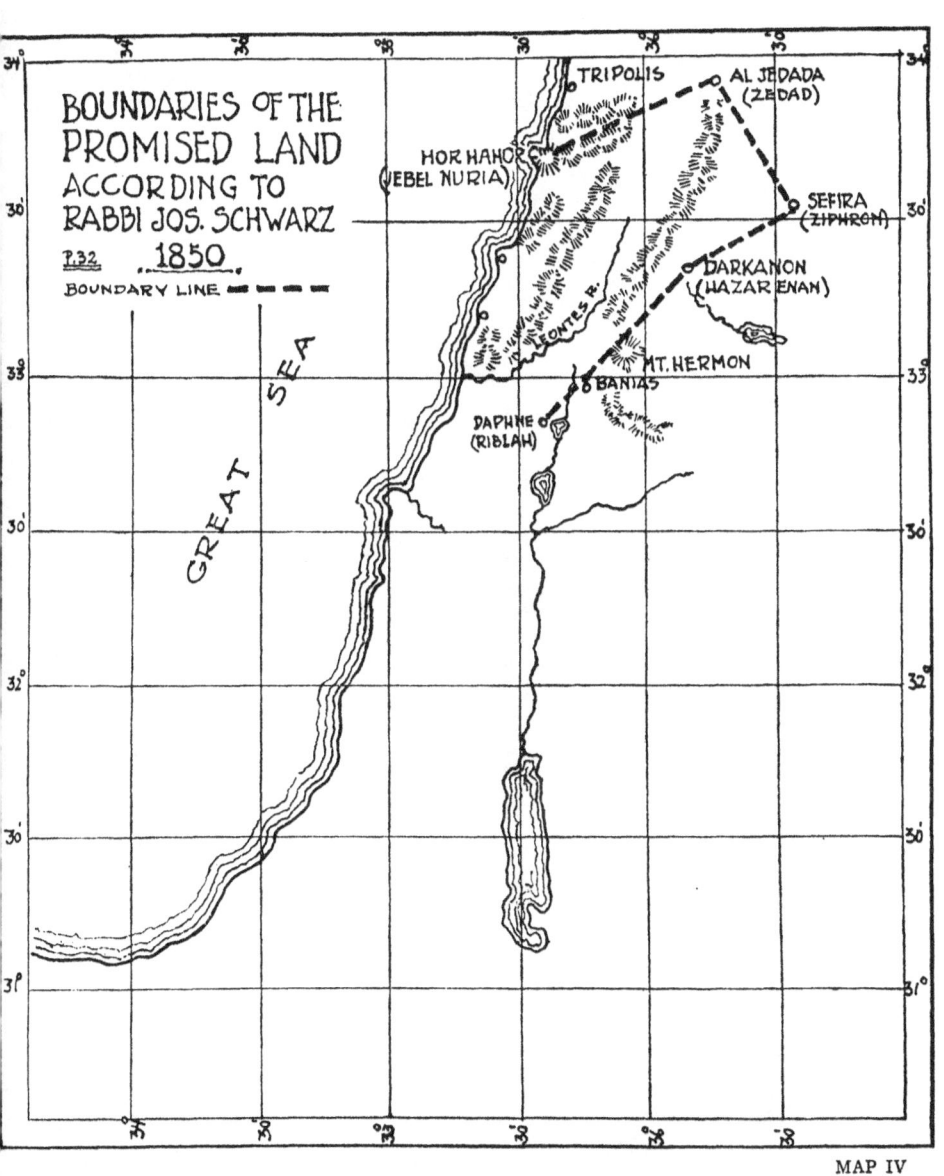

BOUNDARIES OF THE
PROMISED LAND
ACCORDING TO
RABBI JOS. SCHWARZ
P.32 . 1850 .
BOUNDARY LINE ━ ━ ━ ━

TRIPOLIS

AL JEDADA
(ZEDAD)

HOR HAHOR
(JEBEL NURIA)

SEFIRA
(ZIPHRON)

DARKANON
(HAZAR ENAN)

LEONTES R.

MT. HERMON

BANIAS

DAPHNE
(RIBLAH)

GREAT SEA

MAP IV

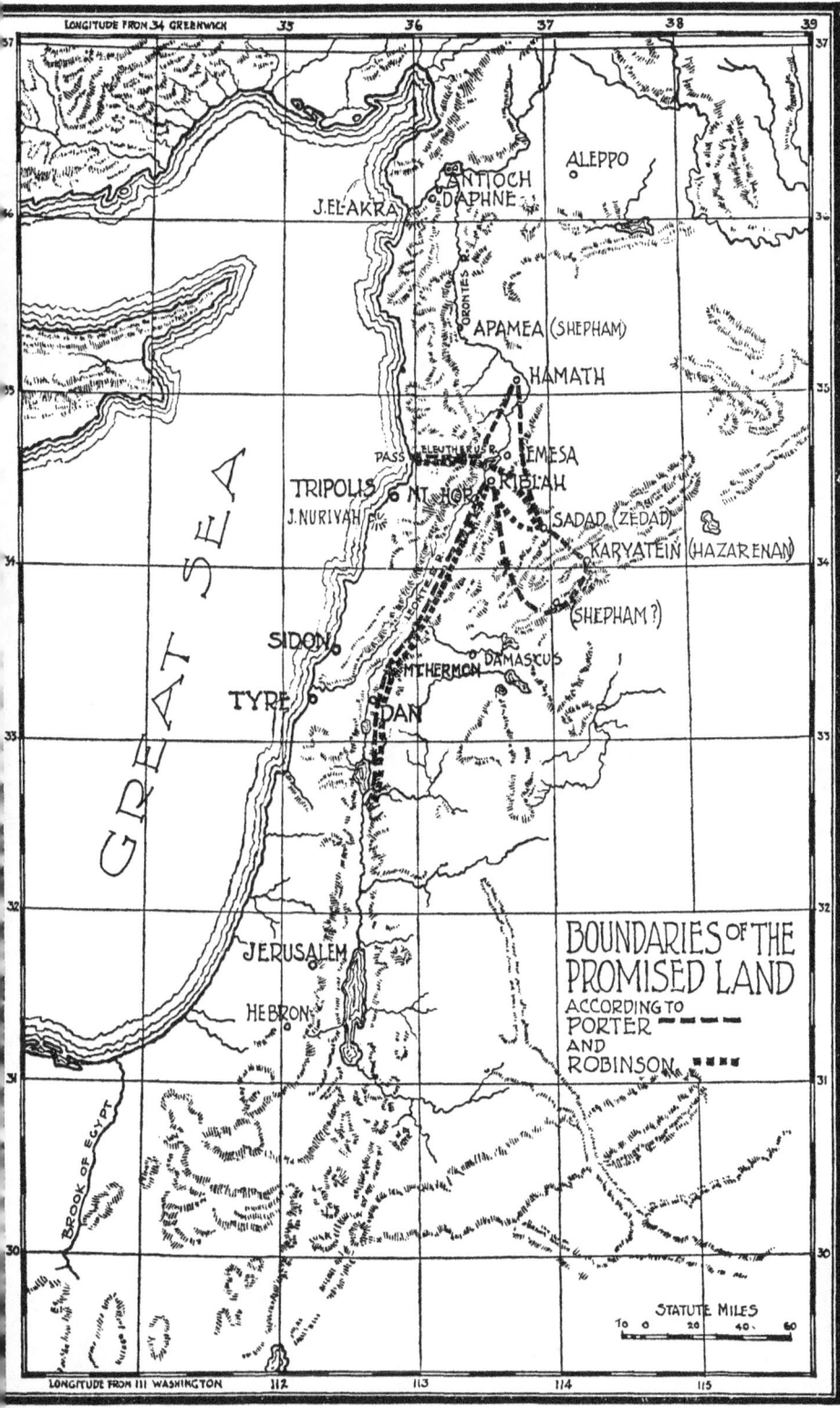

MAP V

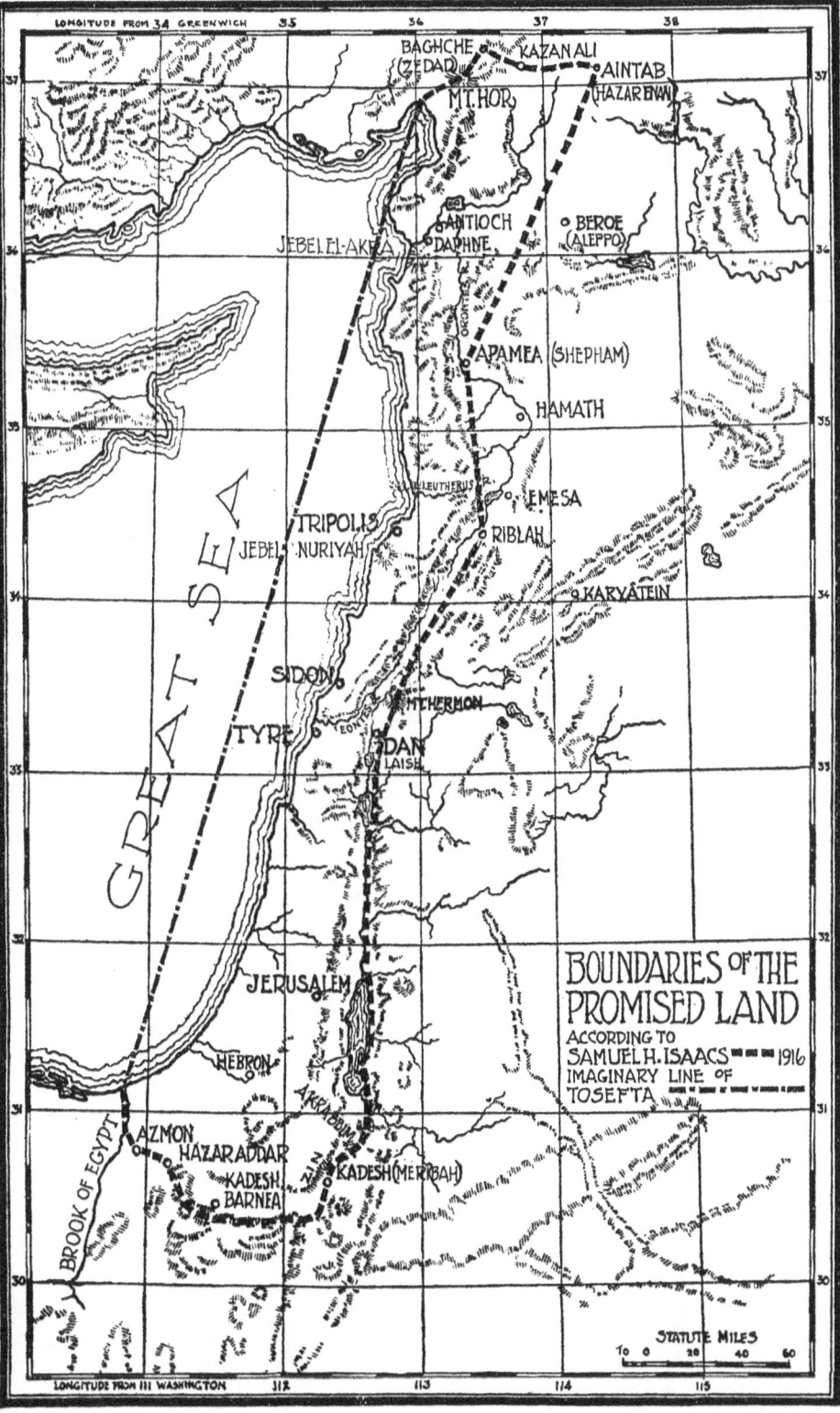

MAP VI

93

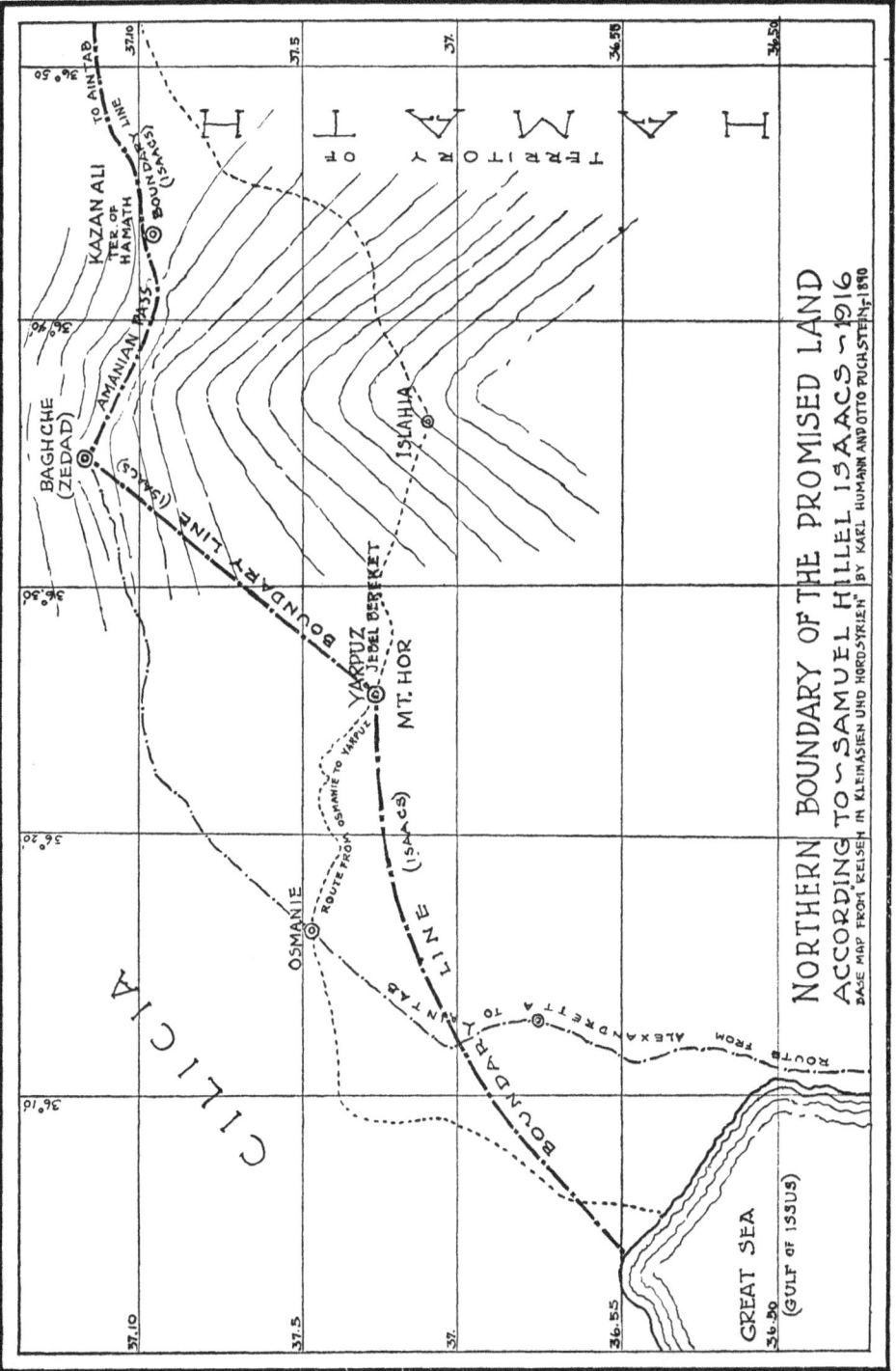

NORTHERN BOUNDARY OF THE PROMISED LAND
ACCORDING TO ~ SAMUEL HILLEL ISAACS ~ 1916
BASE MAP FROM REISEN IN KLEINASIEN UND NORDSYRIEN" BY KARL HUMANN AND OTTO PUCHSTEIN, 1890

MAP VII

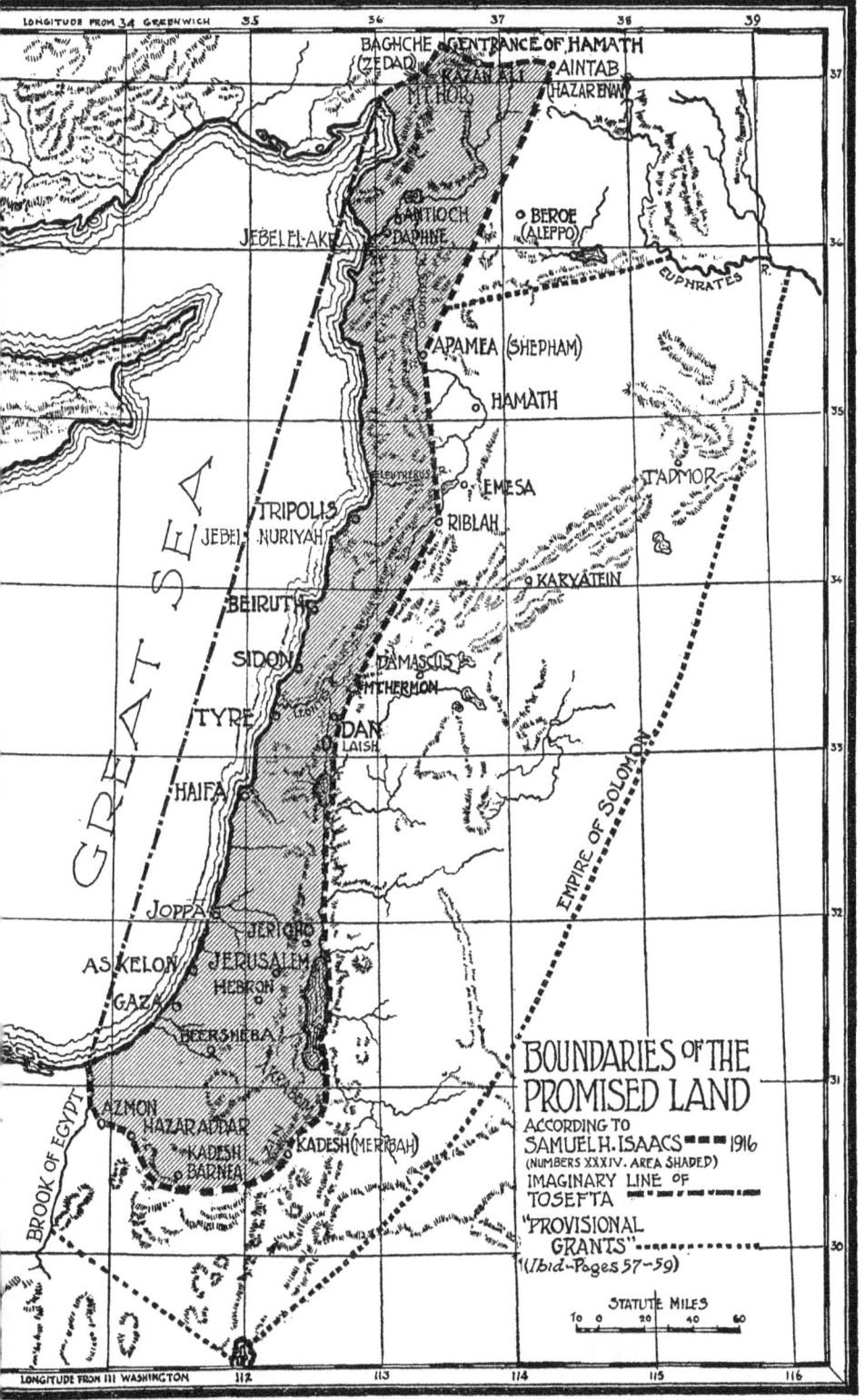

LONGITUDE FROM 34 GREENWICH   35   36   37   38   39

BAGHCHE ·ENTRANCE OF HAMATH
(ZEDAD)
KAZAN ELI ·AINTAB
MT HOR ·HAZAR ENAN

·BEROE
(ALEPPO)
ANTIOCH
JEBEL EL-AKRA ·DAPHNE

EUPHRATES R.

·APAMEA (SHEPHAM)

·HAMATH

GREAT SEA

ELEUTHERUS R.
·EMESA
TRIPOLIS ·TADMOR
JEBEL NURIYAH ·RIBLAH

·KARYATEIN
BEIRUT

SIDON
·DAMASCUS
·MT HERMON
TYRE ·DAN
LAISH
HAIFA

EMPIRE OF SOLOMON

JOPPA
·JERICHO
ASKELON ·JERUSALEM
·HEBRON
GAZA
·BEERSHEBA

BOUNDARIES OF THE PROMISED LAND
ACCORDING TO
SAMUEL H. ISAACS ▪▪▪ 1916
(NUMBERS XXXIV. AREA SHADED)
IMAGINARY LINE OF
TOSEFTA ▪▪▪▪
"PROVISIONAL
GRANTS" ▪▪▪▪
(Ibid-Pages 57-59)

AZMON
HAZAR ADDAR
KADESH ·KADESH (MERIBAH)
BARNEA

BROOK OF EGYPT

STATUTE MILES
10 0   20   40   60

MAP VIII

INDEX

97

INDEX

INDEX